REPAIR

A PROJECT OF THE *BOSTON REVIEW* ARTS IN SOCIETY PROGRAM

D0176656

Editors-in-Chief Deborah Chasman & Joshua Cohen

Managing Editor and Arts Editor Adam McGee

Senior Editor Matt Lord

Engagement Editor Rosie Gillies

Manuscript and Production Editor Hannah Liberman

Contributing Editors Adom Getachew, Walter Johnson, Amy Kapczynski, Robin D. G. Kelley, Lenore Palladino, & Paul Pierson

Contributing Arts Editor Ed Pavlić & Ivelisse Rodriguez

Black Voices in the Public Sphere Fellows Nia T. Evans & Nate File

Editorial Assistants Rosy Fitzgerald & Julia Tong

Fiction and Poetry Contest Administrators Tadhg Larabee & Meghana Mysore

Contest Readers N.T. Arévalo, Neha Bagchi, Catalina Bartlett, Juan Botero, Anna Crumpecker, Jillian Danback, Nathan Dixon, Serenity Dougherty, Lucia Edafioka, Lauren Fadiman, Madeleine Gallo, Tom Guan, Dora Holland, Madison Howard, Charles Hutchison, Jacqueline Kari, Anna Lapera, Max Lesser, Ezra Lebovitz, Kelly McCorkendale, Ben Rutherford, Tanya Shirazi, Jacob Sunderlin, Owen Torrey, & Marie Ungar

Marketing and Development Manager Dan Manchon

Special Projects Manager María Clara Cobo

Finance Manager Anthony DeMusis III

Printer Sheridan PA. Printed and bound in the United States.

Board of Advisors Derek Schrier (Chair), Archon Fung, Deborah Fung, Richard M. Locke, Jeff Mayersohn, Jennifer Moses, Scott Nielsen, Robert Pollin, Rob Reich, Hiram Samel, Kim Malone Scott, & Brandon M. Terry

Interior Graphic Design Zak Jensen & Alex Camlin

Cover Design Alex Camlin

Repair is *Boston Review* Forum 21 (47.1)

Farah Jasmine Griffin's "What Justice Looks Like" is adapted from *Read Until You Understand*, published by W.W. Norton.

Randall Horton's "The Protagonist in Somebody Else's Melodrama" is adapted from *Dead Weight*. Copyright © 2022 Northwestern University. Published 2022 by Northwestern University Press. All rights reserved.

Olúfẹ́mi O. Táíwò's "The Fight for Reparations Cannot Ignore Climate Change" is adapted from *Reconsidering Reparations*. Copyright © 2022 by Olúfẹ́mi O. Táíwò and published by Oxford University Press. All rights reserved.

To become a member, visit bostonreview.net/membership/

For questions about donations and major gifts, contact Dan Manchon, dan@bostonreview.net

For questions about memberships, call 877-406-2443 or email Customer_Service@bostonreview.info.

Boston Review
PO Box 390568
Cambridge, MA 02139

ISSN: 0734-2306 / ISBN: 978-1-946511-68-3

CONTENTS

PART 3: REPAY

EDITORS' NOTE

Adam McGee, Ed Pavlić, & Ivelisse Rodriguez

WE BEAR DEEP WOUNDS, individually and collectively. All have been worsened by a period of destructive politics that left us ill-equipped to respond to a global health catastrophe. As we struggle to recover our footing and grieve our dead, we believe that the arts must have a voice in the conversation about how we heal.

We've organized *Repair* into three sections. Each revolves around a set of themes, without trying to overdetermine how any particular piece is read. In the first section, titled "Repair" like the book, contributors explore sicknesses within the social fabric—from the religious violence that led to the Salem witch trials, to climate catastrophe and the January 6 siege on the Capitol. "Revive" considers racial and colonial violence, and asks us to think about Western medicine—its potentials as well as its failings, and how it can improve in its pursuit of restoring "patients" to health. A major theme of the final section, "Repay," is the aftermath of sexual violence, what it means to take back one's life after such a rupture. As well, the pieces consider gender and racial identity, and claiming the body for oneself.

It's a special pleasure to share work from the winners of *Boston Review*'s two annual writing contests. Yiru Zhang was selected by judge Kali Fajardo-Anstine as the winner of this year's Aura Estrada Short Story Contest. And Sonia Sanchez, our judge for the Annual Poetry Contest, was too enamored of the entries to pick just one; instead, she selected two first-place winners, Adebe DeRango-Adem and Simone Person.

No single text in this volume offers a definitive answer for what it means to repair. But together, they reveal a promising vision for where to go from here.

WE WOULD HEX THE PRESIDENT BUT
Kemi Alabi

our bloom game too strong / altar stays red candle cinnamon-lit
sweet flicker cracking into prance / stays portal door warmed ajar
spell-flung darkward / *would* but we so black we lightless

no mirrors / so touchsoundfood our cedar smoke drumkicks
the body back to gospel / drumsticks the body smacked in mouthfuls
the room perfumes with our funkbrightwild / *would* but our skin yams

plush mothers cackling juice dripping / and this just our first slow branch
ascending / *would* but neighbors to dine and unstranger / rootbind into kin
a nation of misalphaed wolf carcass to climb through / *would* hex their new head

that neverman / rot reeking the soil / but who'd feed these seeds
that wet orange howl just compost slime returning returning
the sky glows red candle / air soots and sludges darkward / still

our funkbrightwild / block by block our tangling tangling
we *would* hex the damned born-dead but billions still alive / cored and alive
threshed concave and still sweet flickers / *would* but *who needs these feasts?*

HOW NATIONS HEAL
Colleen Murphy

IN HIS FIRST SPEECH as president-elect, Joe Biden emphasized the need for national unity and healing. Yet evidence of the depth of existing divisions has only increased since Election Day 2020. In the face of this democratic crisis, what exactly—if anything—will enable Americans to unite and heal?

One common response is to focus squarely on the future and attempt to put the past behind us. Dwelling on the past would only sow further division, on this line of thought. This has been the dominant attitude throughout U.S. history, from settler colonialism and slavery, the Civil War, and Jim Crow to the Vietnam War and the Iraq War. Yet there has always been a strain of U.S. thought that contests these efforts to forget the past, and we hear echoes of that tradition in the present moment.

A chorus of voices, for example, now insists that we hold Trump and members of his administration accountable for pressuring elected officials to change vote tallies, for political corruption, and for his child separation policy at the border. Likewise, calls to invoke the

Twenty-fifth Amendment and impeach Trump followed the mob violence at the Capitol. As so many have pointed out, however, too exclusive a focus on Trump risks treating his administration as an abnormality of U.S. history rather than as a product of conditions that preceded him and that persist now that he is no longer in office. Perhaps most familiar among the larger targets of reckoning is the long legacy of racial injustice. Arguably the largest protest movement in U.S. history, Black Lives Matter, has demanded accountability for police violence and for generations of racial injustice, from slavery to the present day.

This impetus to dig deep into our past is one we should heed: as a society we need to look back first if we are to be able to move forward. This is not only a matter of political strategy in the quest for a just society. It is also a central insight of the ethical framework known as transitional justice, an overlooked but essential resource in the effort to secure the integrity and legitimacy of U.S. democracy.

TRANSITIONAL JUSTICE is both a legal and philosophical theory and a global practice that aims to redress wrongdoing, past and present, in order to vindicate victims, hold perpetrators to account, and transform relationships—among citizens as well as between citizens and public officials. Though it is not as well known in the United States as other paradigms of justice, the framework has been adopted in dozens of countries emerging from periods of war, genocide, dictatorship, and repression, from South Africa to Colombia. As a global practice, the framework began with the recognition that simply moving on hadn't worked.

From the vantage of transitional justice, healing of communities can only occur if we first understand what is damaged, and damage can only be repaired if it is truly acknowledged and addressed. And to help to prevent recurrence of atrocity, we need to draw a line between what was accepted in the past and what will be acceptable in the future. The particular measures used to achieve these aims have ranged from truth commissions and criminal investigations and prosecutions to reparations, lustration (vetting government officials for ties to repressive regimes or activity), and other legal and institutional changes.

To illustrate how transitional justice differs from other frameworks of justice, consider restorative justice, which prioritizes the repair of ruptured relationships among victim, offender, and community caused by wrongdoing. Repair occurs via a model of amends—characteristically via apology and reparations—followed by forgiveness.

Perhaps the greatest problem is that this framework implicitly assumes that there is a shared, morally defensible framework and standards for social interaction already in place. While it may offer valuable guidance for how to respond to wrongful, one-off interactions measured against these standards, it offers flawed guidance for dealing with systemic problems. To see this, consider how forgiveness looks in the context of abusive relationships. To urge victims of domestic violence to forgive—and to let go of their anger—risks encouraging them to capitulate to their own abuse, failing to take seriously the claim the victim has to better treatment, and overlooking the core problem: the abusive terms structuring the relationship itself. Likewise, forgiveness and isolated instances of victim compensation and perpetrator punishment do nothing to change the sources of racial oppression, including—but hardly limited to—racial disparities in health and health care, the persistence of the racial wealth gap, and racially disproportionate police violence.

Transitional justice also distinguishes itself from retributive justice, which demands the punishment of perpetrators of wrongdoing. Theories of retributive justice typically begin with the assumption of state legitimacy and address how the intentional infliction of punishment is compatible with a state's recognition of the equality of all citizens. By contrast, in transitional contexts the question is how to establish the legitimacy of the state and the baseline equality of all citizens in the first place. Retributive theories do not tell us how punishment can do this.

Instead of trying to use familiar theories of justice to deal with systemic wrongdoing, we should instead view transitional justice as a distinctive and irreducible solution. The aim of transitional justice is to fundamentally alter the basic terms of interaction, both horizontally among citizens and vertically between citizens and officials. The ultimate goal of dealing with past wrongdoing is not *only* to satisfy the moral claims of victims and to hold perpetrators to account. It is also to contribute to the transformation of a society so that systemic wrongdoing occurs "never again." For such change to be effective, it must be based on an accurate understanding of the root problems with relationships among members of society. And relationships can be transformed only if we first understand the conditions that enabled injustice to persist and how past wrongs affect present interaction.

WHAT TRANSITIONAL JUSTICE looks like, in practice, has evolved over the past few decades. Colombia provides a helpful illustration. In September 2016 the Colombian government and the Revolutionary Armed Forces of Colombia-People's Army (FARC) signed a historic Final Agreement to End the Armed Conflict and Build a Stable and Lasting Peace (Final Agreement), ending more than fifty years of armed conflict. A modified version of the agreement was ratified by the Colombian Congress in November of that year. The terms of the Final Agreement included explicit provisions for dealing with a variety of wrongdoing committed during the course of the conflict as well as the root causes of the conflict itself. The toll of the conflict was significant: millions forcibly displaced, hundreds of thousands killed, tens of thousands more kidnapped, tortured, or disappeared. Transitional justice processes in the country include a truth commission charged with investigating and explaining the armed conflict, reparations, the Special Unit on the Search for Persons Deemed as Missing, and the Special Jurisdiction for Peace (JEP).

Truth commissions like this one are official bodies established with a mandate to document the occurrence, causes, and consequences of specified human rights violations committed over a delimited period of time. Most commissions also make recommendations for how to prevent similar violations in the future. They collect testimony from witnesses, review documents, and visit sites of violence and typically operate in contexts where the extent of, responsibility for (both individual and institutional), and victims of human rights violations are unclear. Truth commissions provide an official record of violations, establishing the truth about the identity and fate of victims and survivors, the identity of perpetrators, and the causes of wrongdoing.

The JEP, meanwhile, is a set of judicial bodies investigating perpetrators of political crimes such as rebellion as well as war crimes and crimes against humanity. A notable feature of these processes is their wide range of forms of accountability. Perpetrators who confess to political crimes such as rebellion are eligible for amnesty, while those who committed gross human rights violations such as war crimes and crimes against humanity, for political reasons and not for personal enrichment, face a scale of sanctions. Those who fully and immediately confess are eligible to serve five to eight years in zones of restricted liberty—a penalty that is explicitly framed as having a restorative rather than retributive function. Perpetrators who confess after JEP proceedings have begun to face five to eight years in prison, however, and those who do not confess but are ultimately convicted face fifteen to twenty years of imprisonment. Beyond these specific mechanisms, there are provisions for integrating former FARC combatants and for integrating the post-FARC political party through guaranteed political representation in Congress through 2026. There is also a commitment to rural development to address the root causes of conflict and inequality in Colombian society.

What is notable about the Colombian case is that its set of processes for dealing with wrongdoing jointly pursue the central pillars of transitional justice: truth, justice (in the form of accountability), reparations, and institutional reform. Rather than framing the choice between a truth commission and a criminal trial in oppositional terms, the processes are designed to be complementary. Transitional justice theory and practice no longer view the choice societies must face as one *between* truth and justice but as one that pursues truth and justice in tandem. It is important both to tell the truth—to document the pattern and extent of human rights violations and the conditions that enabled their occurrence, as the Colombian truth commission does—and to achieve justice: to hold perpetrators to some kind of account, as the JEP aims to achieve.

The Colombian case also illustrates the profoundly fragile political contexts in which transitional justice is typically pursued. The current president, Iván Duque Márquez, was elected in 2018 on a presidential platform explicitly opposed to specific aspects of the Final Agreement. In particular, he viewed the JEP as failing to achieve a sufficient level of accountability for FARC combatants. Duque's election reflects the fact that the practices of transitional justice are always inherently political. Particular mechanisms of transitional justice are controversial and contestable in part because they are necessarily imperfect. Not all perpetrators and victims are addressed; those who are will almost certainly not see perfect justice; nor are perpetrators punished commensurate with what retribution would seem to mandate or deterrence would seem to require. But the perfect should not be the enemy of the good, and transitional justice is the best solution we have for achieving a fundamental transformation of social and political relationships after systemic wrongdoing.

THE IDEA THAT THE SAME FRAMEWORK for healing conflict-torn Colombia should be implemented in the United States is sure to strike many Americans as implausible. Underpinning this skepticism is often a distinctive form of U.S. exceptionalism. In defining away any wrongdoing as "un-American," or in limiting its range to outright civil war or widespread armed conflict, such reactions obscure distinctively U.S. failures, obscure the need for distinctively U.S. change, and prevent us from learning from other countries. Reckoning with U.S. injustice requires humility and a willingness to be open to the possibility that we could have done—and should now do—better. Transitional justice offers a global and comparative lens through which to situate problems specific to the United States and from which to evaluate proposed solutions.

To some extent, the 2020 elections and Trump era have blunted that sense of exceptionalism. Moreover, amidst widespread disagreement about just about everything, few Americans would dispute the claim that our society is characterized by deep, and deepening, political divisions. Our institutional fragility creates precisely the kind of serious existential uncertainty characteristic of transitional contexts.

Yet exceptionalism persists and has been on display in many reactions to the storming of the Capitol, which have emphasized that "this is not who we are" and characterized the violence as a feature of "banana republics" or the "Third World." Of a piece with such reactions is a common conflation of our ideals with our practice, which is then used to discredit any proposed critique. To focus on where we have, in fact, done wrong or failed to live up to our ideals as a nation is not to reject those ideals; indeed, very often the ideals themselves provide the basis for explaining our failure. Pointing this out is not to reject our ideals, but rather to reject U.S. acts that do not live up to them.

Once we set such exceptionalism aside, we are prepared to see that the similarities between the United States and other transitional contexts run deep indeed. (In fact, aspects of transitional justice already have a history in certain U.S. contexts, such as the national Commission on Wartime Relocation and Internment of Civilians, carried out in the 1980s to address the interment of Japanese Americans during World War II, and the Illinois Torture Inquiry and Relief Commission, initiated in 2009 to respond to decades of torture enacted by Chicago Police.) Deciding whether transitional justice is necessary for a community requires examining what I call "the circumstances of transitional justice." Transforming political relationships becomes morally necessary and is practically possible under these circumstances.

One circumstance is *serious existential uncertainty*, which captures the fragility of political contexts in which the political future becomes profoundly unclear. Since the unfounded challenges to the 2020 election results and Capitol riots, for example, peaceful and democratic transitions of power can no longer be taken as a given. Moreover, like other paradigm transitional societies, the United States is also marked by *pervasive structural inequality*, in our context heavily shaped by race. Structural inequality explains how certain groups of citizens are disproportionately unable to avoid poverty, participate in political and economic processes, or shape the rules and norms for interaction. Structural inequality runs deep both throughout U.S. history and in the present day. Examples include the persistent racial wealth gap, basically unchanged since the end of Jim Crow; the long history of voter suppression and disenfranchisement targeting Black citizens; and the disproportionate burden of COVID-19 (in terms of mortality, job loss, etc.) borne by Black and Indigenous people.

The third key circumstance is *normalized political wrongdoing*: when human rights violations perpetrated by state actors become a basic fact of life for members of certain groups. The racially disproportionate effect of police violence is just one such case. Though they make up only 13 percent of the population, Black Americans make up more than 25 percent of police shooting victims. Pervasive structural inequality and normalized political wrongdoing make the transformation of political relationships among citizens and between citizens and officials morally necessary.

OF COURSE, just because we need transitional justice in the United States in no way guarantees we will pursue it. Efforts to downplay or sideline concerns with the historical and abiding injustices perpetrated against various marginalized communities—especially communities of color —pose one of the greatest obstacles to national unity. To understand how to combat denial, we need first to understand the forms it takes.

In his 2001 study *States of Denial: Knowing about Atrocities and Suffering*, psychologist Stanley Cohen identifies three forms that denial of injustice can take. The first is literal denial, where basic facts are disputed. Consider Trump's 2020 Presidential Executive Order 13950 and a follow-up Memo from the Executive Branch Office of Management and Budget to heads of Executive Departments and Agencies. Both engaged in literal denial by suggesting that discussion of any racism or evil actions in our past is "propaganda." More specifically, EO 13950 characterized as mere ideology the claim that the United States "is grounded in hierarchies based on collective social and political identities rather than in the inherent and equal dignity of every person as an individual." It stipulated as false that anyone on the basis of their race could oppress or benefit from racialized segregation or slavery, contending that such ideas are grounded in a "destructive ideology" and "misrepresentations of our country's history and its role in the world."

The second form Cohen discusses is interpretive denial, where an act or state of affairs that is wrong is redescribed so as to downplay wrongfulness. A striking example is Senator Tom Cotton's July 2020 characterization of slavery as a "necessary evil." Cotton's words captured a common view among conservatives, downplaying the gravity of the wrong of slavery and implicitly seeking to justify, rather than repudiate, that part of our nation's history. Likewise, the *New York Times*'s 1619 Project, which "aims to reframe the country's history by placing the consequences of slavery and the contributions of black Americans at the very center of our national narrative," has generated pushback that goes beyond scholarly disputes to call into question the legitimacy of centering Black lives and experiences and centuries of slavery. This extreme form of repudiation is different in kind from the criticism about specific conclusions or pieces of evidence to which any research project is rightly subject; it reflects a form of interpretive denial regarding the significance and centrality of white supremacy and racial injustice in the United States.

Cohen calls the third form of denial "implicatory": acknowledging something is happening but refusing to acknowledge its significance. Wrongdoing may become so normalized that it is no longer the subject of outrage. Other forms of implicatory denial involve a rejection or displacement of responsibility for wrongdoing. Following the mob attack on the Capitol, for example, many in conservative media shifted responsibility from Trump supporters to outside "agitators" who "don't look like Trump supporters."

All three forms of denial are examples of what philosopher Tommie Shelby calls ideological racism, in which commonly held beliefs and judgments distort social reality in ways that lead to enduring injustice in social relationships. As Cohen explains, official denial is successful only when there is a willing audience. "Denials draw on shared cultural vocabularies to be credible," he writes. "They may also be shared in another powerful sense: the commitment between people—whether partners (folie à deux) or an entire organization—to back up and collude in each other's denials." Such denial, undergirded by white anxiety, deepened and worsened during the Trump presidency, but its roots stretch back throughout U.S. history. The most effective way to counter these insidious forms of denial is to embrace the practices of transitional justice. As Wesley Morris wrote in the *New York Times* in July 2020:

> This Moment of historic holding to account, of looking inward,
> deserves a commensurate, totalizing event that explains what is

being reckoned with, demanded and hoped for, an experience that rubs between its fingers the earth upon which all those toppled monuments had so brazenly stood. The Moment warrants a depth of conversation the United States has never had. It demands truth and reconciliation. . . . Truth and reconciliation is a death and a birth, accordingly arduous, tense, procedural, affirming, painful. . . . The Moment demands that we summon the courage to put ourselves through it. At last.

FOR ALL THESE REASONS, there is growing emphasis among scholars and practitioners of transitional justice that it is urgently needed in the United States. Measures taken in recent years parallel that growing consensus, including the Maine Wabanaki-State Child Welfare Truth & Reconciliation Commission (which operated from 2013 to 2015), the Equal Justice Initiative's National Memorial for Peace and Justice (which opened in 2018 in Montgomery, Alabama), the Maryland Lynching Truth and Reconciliation Commission (established in 2019 by House Bill 307), New York City's Racial Justice and Reconciliation Commission, and a reparations program for Black residents passed by the city council of Asheville, North Carolina.

As these calls and efforts grow, the scope of U.S. transitional justice—the specific wrongs it confronts—as well as the design and implementation of concrete measures must be informed by a variety of stakeholders, including scholars, activists, practitioners, and members of affected communities. On the issue of racial justice specifically, it is critical that scholarship merge two complementary sources of insight that are rarely in conversation: the scholarship on civil rights and Black political thought, on the one hand, and scholarship on transitional justice, on the other. Context shapes what processes are most needed and what form measures like truth commissions should take. Deep, context-specific knowledge is critical to developing appropriate and effective responses to racial injustice. For more than a century, scholars of civil rights and Black political thought have diagnosed the sources of racial injustice economically, politically, and in terms of criminal justice in the United States. They have outlined mechanisms for its redress, including but not limited to reparations. Deep knowledge of how racial injustice operates and the form it takes is essential for developing prescriptions.

At the same time, we must bear in mind that there is no simple formula for what set of processes should be used to pursue transitional justice. Nor is there a short and simple route to success in transforming political relationships. Empirical research documents the tangible impact measures such as truth commissions, lustration, and institutional reform can have in contributing to democratic stability and providing a foundation for building more just societies. Such research also underscores limitations in the existing transitional justice practice in dealing with structural and racial injustice, which the United States must avoid. Most fundamentally, transformational change is a generational project requiring ongoing political will beyond the mandate of specific transitional justice processes, as the experience in Germany shows. A single truth and reconciliation commission cannot by itself transform the lives of marginalized and victimized individuals and political relationships more broadly. Transformation requires multiple processes and robust institutional reform.

However these practices ultimately take shape, it is essential that we begin to have these conversations among the necessary stakeholders and at the highest levels of government, now. A national framework for transitional justice is needed to complement isolated local efforts, both those to come and those already underway. To facilitate this, Biden could establish a commission on transitional justice and build a relationship with the United Nations Special Rapporteur on the Promotion of Truth, Justice, Reparation and Guarantees of Non-Recurrence. We must acknowledge that decades of efforts to put the past behind us have failed. Far from a framework applicable only elsewhere, transitional justice provides the necessary resources to reckon honestly with U.S. wrongdoing—and to help transform our society in ways that finally live up to the ideals we profess.

WHAT JUSTICE LOOKS LIKE
Farah Jasmine Griffin

IT WAS AT A SUMMER COOKOUT that I recall first seeing the scars, dark brown, raised, and thick, that poured down Uncle Pitt's back. He sat on a folding chair, laughing. He laughed a lot, and occasionally danced, grabbing my mother's hand and twirling with her in what seemed to me an old-fashioned partner dance. Having been raised as a proper Black child, I neither stared nor pointed, but I was transfixed by the scars and kept the image at the forefront of my mind until I could ask my mother about them. "Mommy, what is that on Uncle Pitt's back? Is he hurt?" She responded, "No, he is fine. See how happy he is?"

Later she told me that sometimes when people were imprisoned, scientists and doctors conducted experiments on them in exchange for things like cigarettes. Uncle Pitt had been "experimented on." She said this as a matter of fact, if with a tinge of sadness. She said it in that same tone she used whenever she had to reveal something harsh. It was as if the tone would soften the blow of the knowledge she revealed.

I knew Uncle Pitt had been incarcerated. Aunt Eartha wrote letters to him and to her oldest son, who was in the military. On our side of the family, each generation had at least one young man who had "done time" and at least one who went to the military. My maternal grandfather served in the military. Daddy was in the Navy and later did four months for drug possession, before I was born. Uncle Pitt had been in the Army. Of my male cousins, one had done a little time for gang fighting with a BB gun; his brother had gone to Vietnam. Of my two nephews, one served time for manslaughter before he turned twenty and the other went into the Air Force right out of high school. All of them, whether on the right side or wrong side of the law, had encounters with the police, who stopped and questioned, sometimes harassed, and at least once brutally beat them. It was a hated but almost expected occurrence in our lives. At any given time, we were helping fund someone's bail, or offering support at court, paying lawyers and bail bondsmen, receiving and writing letters to our loved ones there. That was the plight of our men. None of them spoke to the women or children about their time in prison. I hope they spoke to each other.

As a girl, I knew that men I loved sometimes ended up in prison. I knew that some of them might have done something to be there, but incarceration didn't have to be an indication of guilt. There were many innocents behind bars. Interestingly, though we all knew someone who had done or was doing time, we also knew that many of our neighbors who had been victims of crime rarely even bothered to call the police.

If I was haunted by the sight of Uncle Pitt's scars, other incidents haunted me more: the frequent occurrences of sexual assault, including gang rape. When such instances transpired, families rarely called the police. They feared girls would be further victimized by them and were almost certain her assailant would not be convicted.

Although the failure to report sexual crimes was presented as an effort to protect the victim, I also understood it as a failure to fully value the lives of Black girls. I believed one of the only things standing between me and such victimization was the protection of the men in my family. If I had been assaulted, I assume but am not sure my family would have called the police; they too doubted the ability or willingness of the police to deliver justice. However, this I knew, deep in my bones: if my assailant had been known to my family, he would have been maimed or murdered.

In her first memoir, *I Know Why the Caged Bird Sings* (1969), Maya Angelou reveals that in all likelihood, her uncles murdered the man who molested her as a girl. Although separated by time and location, I recognized that moment as one that could have been mirrored in my own life. In the world in which I was raised, prisons rarely offered rehabilitation and courts did not serve justice. Whites didn't do time for harming Blacks; Blacks were unjustly imprisoned. Justice as we understood it was Divine—God would take care of it; or it was retributive, meted out by gangs, friends, and family members.

What is the nature and possibility of justice for the crimes of racism, slavery, segregation, and mass incarceration that Black people have experienced in the United States? What does justice look like for centuries of systemic abuse and violence enacted by a society built upon withholding justice from Black people? In all of her novels, Toni Morrison contemplates the nature and practice of justice.

Throughout *Song of Solomon* (1977), Morrison explores the meaning of and quest for justice. She is especially interested in the nature of justice and its relationship to vengeance and history, retribution and repair. Significantly, most of the discussions about justice take place between the novel's men. The first and most explicit discussion occurs in the barbershop. The narrator tells us:

> A young Negro boy had been found stomped to death in Sunflower County, Mississippi. There were no questions about who stomped him—his murderers had boasted freely—and there were no questions about the motive. The boy had whistled at some white woman, refused to deny he had slept with others and was a Northerner visiting the South. His name was Till.

The statement does a great deal of work. It declares the matter-of-factness of the murder. It is spoken like it might be a common occurrence. There is no mystery to be solved. The culprits are known. They feel neither remorse nor guilt. They do not fear arrest, trial, or conviction. The dialogue that follows occurs in the shadow of Emmett Till's murder in August 1955. Till is the Black fourteen-year-old from Chicago who is falsely accused of molesting a white woman whose husband and brother-in-law then brutally murder him. The conversation that ensues illustrates the diversity of opinion and ideology in the Black community. The more conservative speaker almost blames the teenager for provoking his own death. His open defiance of the rules governing contact between Black men and white women constitutes a refusal to stay within the confines that the Jim Crow South sets for Black people. Another man counters by noting that Till was murdered for daring to act like a man.

No matter their politics, each man in the barbershop knows that his skin color constitutes guilt in the eyes of whites and that they are all vulnerable to any white vigilante without recourse to justice. The very arbitrariness of white power is what makes it so frightening. At any given time, in any given place, they too might share Till's fate.

Guitar, a militant young Black man, member of a vigilante group that seeks eye-for-an-eye justice, articulates an argument based on the historical truth of justice denied. He says:

> We poor people, Milkman. I work at an auto plant. The rest of us barely eke out a living. Where's the money, the state, the country to finance our justice? You say Jews try their catches in a court. Do we have a court? Is there one courthouse in one city in the country where a jury would convict them? There are places right now where a Negro still can't testify against a white man. Where the judge, the jury, the court, are legally bound to ignore anything a Negro has to say. What that means is that a Black man is a victim of a crime only when a white man says he is.

In an era when the murderers of too many Black Americans walk free, readers will feel the ongoing truth of Guitar's assertion. Morrison demonstrates the persistence of injustice through time and place, past and present, North and South. The only justice Morrison's male characters can imagine is vengeance. Most advocate survival over revenge; in so doing they forego seeking justice.

Morrison offers another possibility through Circe, a midwife and servant who lives in the ruins of a plantation mansion once owned by a white family, the Butlers. Circe is the subversive agent who undermines everything her white employers lived and died for. She is over a hundred years old, and her face is a map of wrinkles. After the murder of protagonist Milkman's paternal grandfather, Macon Dead, Sr., Circe rescues, hides, and takes care of his two children. She takes from the Butler's wealth, made by slavery and then by stealing the land of freedmen, to care for the orphaned children of one of their victims. She feeds them, provides them shelter and love, hides them from harm, and sends them on their way. Their problem becomes her problem. She enacts an ethic of care that helps ensure their well-being and their ability to become self-sufficient.

Morrison's Circe, like Homer's, serves as Milkman's escort and as a guide to the spirits of the dead, in that she guides Milkman to seek his family's history and, consequently, his own identity. She is a healer, nurturer, and protector, but she is also a justice seeker. She helps to bring a long-term sense of justice into being. It is not justice for those who were the immediate recipients of harm, nor does it punish those who have caused the harm. But it helps to create a more just society for the progeny of both.

With their large columned mansion, the Butlers laid claim to a classical past, but Morrison assures us it is the enslaved whose roots are more ancient than Eden and whose progeny reach into the present (though perhaps not into the future). Western democracies like the United States claim a cultural, philosophical, and political lineage that links them to the ancient Greeks and Romans. Through Circe,

Morrison reminds us that those ancient civilizations were also slave societies. In Morrison's hands the progeny of the enslaved and their quest for justice outlast the material wealth that their labor helped to create. The grand plantation, an ode to temples of the past, is now, like those of the ancient world, a ruin.

There will be no romantic plantation tours at the Butler place. Circe does not act out of a love of whiteness, nor out of loyalty. Neither does she act out of revenge. She lives with a patient sense of justice, a kind of divine retribution, and for the return of the Black son. She gains pleasure not by killing the Butlers, but by watching their monument to history and greed decay from within and bearing witness to its ruin. As Circe explains: "They [the Butlers] loved this place. Loved it. . . . Stole for it, lied for it, killed for it. But I'm the one left. Me and the dogs. . . . Everything in this world they lived for will crumble and rot." What doesn't rot on its own, she will allow the dogs to destroy. "Ha! And I want to see it all go, make sure it does go, and that nobody fixes it up."

Through Circe, Morrison juxtaposes the Odyssey's version of the Quest narrative with a quest that will yield a suppressed history, narrate the lives of those who have been victims of the West, and thoroughly question the patriarchy by insisting on a reconstructed masculinity at quest's end.

In *Song of Solomon*, Morrison explores the potential of retributive justice, which she rejects in favor of a long-term divine justice toward which the universe bends. In *Home* (2012), however, Morrison turns most fully to the potential of restorative justice to be a guiding principle of a society governed by an ethic of care. There is nothing that can make up for the crimes against her victimized characters. In her model, the offender is not reconciled with the victim, but the victim is cared for and embraced by the community. And witnessing this, the victim's brother, who in another instance has been an offender, must come to terms with the trauma he has caused and do something ethically productive. As a result, at novel's end a victim and a victimizer are transformed.

Set in the 1950s, *Home* is the story Frank Money, an African American veteran traumatized by his experiences in the Korean War, who receives word that his younger sister Cee is in harm's way in Georgia, and sets out to rescue her. Cee has been working as a domestic servant for a white doctor, Beauregard Scott. Unbeknownst to Cee, Scott is a eugenicist who "occasionally performed abortions on society ladies," and who is seeking to improve the speculum, mutilating a number of poor Black women in the process. Cee quickly becomes victim to Scott's experimentation.

Frank carries his sister in his arms until they can hire a hack to convey them to their small hometown, Lotus. There he hands her over to Miss Ethel and a band of local women, who undertake the work of healing her. At no point does anyone call the police, nor do they issue a complaint to a medical board. These are not options that will do Cee any good, since they won't render justice to her.

First, they tend to her bodily wounds. The women take turns providing her medicinal herbs and potions. Cee's healing includes be-ing "sun-smacked, which meant spending at least one hour a day with her legs spread open to the blazing sun." The women believe access to the sun's healing powers provides "a permanent cure. The kind beyond human power."

The ten days exposed to the sun is a ritual, an absorption of energy to combat evil and harm. At the end of two months in their care, "Cee was different." These women confront illness as an enemy they must vanquish. Their care is without sentiment, and it certainly holds no pity. As Cee heals with help from their potions and food, they bring her embroidery and crocheting to do and, when she's ready, they invite her into their quilting circle. Finally, when she is healed to their liking, Miss Ethel tells her:

> Look to yourself. You free. Nothing and nobody is obliged to save you but you. Seed your own land. You young and a woman and there's serious limitation in both, but you a person too. Don't let . . . some trifling boyfriend and certainly no devil doctor decide who you are. That's slavery. Somewhere inside you is that free person I'm talking about. Locate her and let her do some good in the world.

Freedom lies not in her social condition but in her self-perception. She must understand herself to be a self-reliant, self-possessed grown woman before she can fully enter, as an equal, the community of women who cared for and healed her. She must have a sense of herself beyond her victimization so as never again to give herself over to those who would further victimize her. Freedom here is a mental state, one that she must claim for herself.

Morrison identifies the women's work to heal Cee as an "instance of innate group compassion." The women's ethic of care gives Cee her self, transformed, wounded, but standing strong. Like many Black and poor women in the South, she has been sterilized by a doctor without her knowledge and consent. She carries the burden of that loss within her, and yet she leaves the women stronger, economically self-sufficient (she sells her quilts to visiting tourists), and no longer in need of her brother's rescuing:

> Frank didn't know what took place during those weeks at Miss Ethel's house surrounded by those women with seen-it-all eyes. . . . They delivered unto him a Cee who would never again need his hand over her eyes or his arms to stop her murmuring bones.

In *Home*, there can be no justice for what Dr. Scott has taken from Cee, especially as it is unlikely that what he did to her even counted as a crime. In *Intimate Justice: The Black Female Body and the Body Politic* (2016), political theorist Shatema Threadcraft reminds us that Black women who suffered forced sterilization at the hands of the state are largely responsible for the shift in feminist language from a right to abortion to "reproductive rights." So pervasive was this practice that it became commonplace and was nicknamed a "Mississippi appendectomy." And it was legal. Threadcraft wonders: "What, in this instance, does justice require?" The project of intimate justice, she writes, "is still incomplete."

There is no movement demanding justice for Cee, just a community of women that heals her wounds, teaches her how to incorporate her physical and emotional scars into the woman she has become, and sends her off to fulfill her purpose to do some good in the world. The women model a kind of behavior and ethical practice that lays the foundation for her transformation. They do not invite her victimizer into the restorative justice process or into their community. And yet, their community offers healing to those who have victimized others.

As we learn, part of Frank's mental trauma is a result of his own horrific action during his time in Korea. He is broken from the guilt he bears. Returning to Lotus to rescue his sister restores him as well. Before returning home, he sees the world in black and white, but once he has delivered his sister, he notices, "It was so bright, brighter than he remembered." He notes "marigolds, nasturtiums, dahlias. Crimson, purple, pink, and China blue. Had these trees always been this deep, deep green?" Clarity and an appreciation for the world's beauty return to him after he acts out of love to save his sister.

Morrison has suggested that the very act of putting stories of suffering on display is necessary to acquire justice. Restorative justice seeks to offer repair, to put things as they should be. Many progressive thinkers and activists have argued for restorative justice to replace the punitive paradigm, which governs so much of U.S. society. Others are beginning to turn from restoration to transformation. Activist and scholar Zaheer Ali writes:

> If things are restored back to the way they used to be, the same arrangements of power, the same relationships, the same mindsets, etc., is that really justice? But if we think about *transformative justice* as a means by which to create a space that allows people to exercise agency to make new (and better) decisions in their lives—maybe that is closer to justice.

The novel can raise questions about the possibilities and goals of justice. It allows us to imagine what a society governed by an ethic of care—devoted to restoring and repairing those who have been harmed, giving them the space for transformation—might look like. It is not easy, it does not offer the possibility of a cure, but it encourages healing. The scar is still there. It becomes a part of the new person, who is hurt but not broken. As such she can go on living a productive life devoted to goodness and breaking a cycle of harm.

In an interview, activist and philosopher Angela Davis says: "I think that restorative justice is a really important dimension of the process of living the way we want to live in the future. . . . We have to begin that process of creating the society we want to inhabit right now." This, I think, is the work of the novel, especially in Morrison's hands. Her late fiction imagines worlds that were, and in so doing, provides a template for what might be. Interestingly in Morrison's case, achieving justice is secondary to the acquisition of self-knowledge. She asserts that "a satisfactory or good ending for me is when the protagonist learns something vital and morally insightful that she or he did not know at the beginning." I wonder if the acquisition of self-knowledge might not be the result of a process of restorative justice.

By novel's end, Frank and Cee stand like the tree with which Morrison closes the novel, a sweet bay tree with olive-green leaves, "hurt right down the middle." This image, of the tree, scarred but not broken, sustains me. I hold on to the possibility of communal love and care in the ongoing struggle for justice. I hold on to it even amid ongoing trauma, in large part because I have been the beneficiary of transformative care. It is this love for those denied justice that motivates us to continue to seek it. Our movements hold the victims of injustice dear, say their names, weep for them, and struggle to hold those who caused them harm responsible, to transform the society that allowed for their victimization. Theologian Serene Jones writes: "Mercy grants freedom from the bondage of harms. Justice is the struggle to make sure those harms stop."

The struggle for justice is ongoing. In the meantime, we work to heal, love, and transform the world into a more just place.

THREE POEMS
Donia Elizabeth Allen

WHAT SORCERIES

I use
spirits. I like

to see
what flares up.

I goe in—
no question

or intention—
& I wait,

I let fire
flower

then consort
with its blue

flames,
its sooty wings.

DID YOU NEVER PRACTISE WITCHCRAFT IN YOUR OWNE COUNTRY

I apprentise to water
hurtling over dank rocks

to sudden gusts
& the leaves thay sweep skyward

like hundreds & hundreds of dry
hands clapping

I believ in swaying
cattails in July in evening

heat as it croons
hydrangea to dust

I come from silt & exposed
roots I practise mist

from the rapids
rising into pines

I HEARD LAST NIGHT A KIND OF THUNDRING

You speak of dunes,
& plovers

darting in & outt
of swooning

beach grass.
You speak of broken

shells & surf lashing
clay clifs.

I wade in. I am
nott afrayde of swells

that lift mee
off my feet,

or of a strong
undertow, or sea glass.

Author's Note: These poems are inspired by the 1692 Salem witch trials. The titles come from court records, which have been collected and edited by Paul Boyer and Stephen Nissenbaum in The Salem Witchcraft Papers *(1977) and, more recently, by Bernard Rosenthal in* Records of the Salem Witch-Hunt *(2009). The poems are also informed by Boyer and Nissenbaum's* Salem Possessed: The Social Origins of Witchcraft *(1974).*

Allen

THE FIGHT FOR REPARATIONS CANNOT IGNORE CLIMATE CHANGE

Olúfẹ́mi O. Táíwò

IN RECENT YEARS there has been a resurgence of interest in reparations. Perhaps most familiarly, Ta-Nehisi Coates's influential 2014 essay in the *Atlantic*, "The Case for Reparations," set off a firestorm of reactions across the political spectrum, culminating years later in a "historic" congressional hearing in 2019. In the wake of George Floyd's murder and the rebellions of 2020, reparations programs task forces have launched in the city of Detroit and state of California while a housing payment program launched in Evanston. And in 2021 House Resolution 40—introduced every year in Congress since John Conyers, Jr., first introduced it in 1989, and calling for a commission to study reparations for slavery—finally passed through the Judiciary Committee for full consideration on the House floor.

But what exactly does the call for reparations demand, and what kind of political movement does it entail? The label has been applied to a vast array of different programs and policies, from direct cash payments to African Americans to symbolic apologies, creations of museums and sites of spiritual recognition, and academic studies about the nature of systemic racism. In a 2016 essay, political scientist Adolph Reed, Jr., took aim at this feature of the call for reparations, describing it as a blend of "material, symbolic, and psychological components." Reed thinks this ambiguity is a liability, since elites can exploit the demand by choosing the version of reparations that is cheapest for them: the symbolic. More important, Reed contends, overinvestment in symbolic reparations could detract energy and resources from an alternative, preferable political project: "building broad solidarity across race, gender, and other identities around shared concerns of daily life" like "access to quality health care, the right to a decent and dignified livelihood, affordable housing, quality education for all." Reed thus warns that the call for reparations for some distracts from a more worthy political project that would provide justice for all—an objection also voiced during the 2019 House hearing.

But what if the project for reparations was the project for "safer neighborhoods and better schools," for a "less punitive justice system," for "the right to a decent and dignified livelihood"? Responding to Reed in *Dissent* in 2019, African American studies scholar Keeanga-Yamahtta Taylor pointed out that the struggle to build a just social system can't be won solely through "universal" programs addressing common problems. Taylor gives the example of the large disparity rate in maternal mortality between Black mothers and white mothers: the accumulated history of disparate and discriminatory treatment and policy means that not all of the relevant social problems are, in fact, common to both. To build a just health care system, we would have to address both lack of access due to unjust economic structures and lack of access due to unfair gender- and race-based discrimination. From the point of view of building a just health care system, these goals aren't substitutes for each other; they are complementary.

Though it is less well elaborated in today's popular debates, this understanding of reparations—one that sees it as central to the expansive project of building a more just world, not just as a material or symbolic mechanism of redress for past harms—has a long legacy. This vision is worth recovering and integrating with other important political movements today, above all the global struggle for climate justice.

THERE IS AMPLE FOOTING, both in theory and in practice, for widening the scope of our conversations about reparations in this way. In his historical study of the Black radical imagination, *Freedom Dreams* (2002), historian Robin D. G. Kelley notes that the demand for reparations "was never entirely, or even primarily, about money." Instead, it was

> about social justice, reconciliation, reconstructing the internal life of black America, and eliminating institutional racism. This is why reparations proposals from black radical movements focus less on individual payments than on securing funds to build autonomous black institutions, improving community life, and in some cases establishing a homeland that will enable African Americans to develop a political economy geared more toward collective needs than toward accumulation.

This view—constructive in outlook and global in ambition—has a particularly useful antecedent in mid-century struggles for independence. As historian Adom Getachew shows in her recent book *Worldmaking after Empire: The Rise and Fall of Self-Determination* (2019), the wave of decolonization movements that crested toward the end of World War II forced new political questions onto the world stage. Prominent figures in the growing global anticolonial movement demanded the institutionalization of self-determination as a political principle of the United Nations, and worked to form regional political blocs for mutual aid and uplift. They also insisted on a New International Economic Order with a different set of rules than what had arisen from colonial domination and the capitalist economy that emerged from it: what I call "global racial empire." They imagined new institutions, different relationships between countries, and also, crucially, the most recognizable aspect of reparations politics: redistribution of global wealth, from the First World (back) to the Third World.

These activists weren't just fighting *against* the structures of colonial domination and racial apartheid; they were also trying to build a more just world on a planetary scale. Unfortunately, they did not succeed: the end of the Cold War, the disciplining of the newly independent states, and the corresponding defeat of radical politics around the globe produced struggles for justice that often set their sights much lower. But any politically serious reparations project—at least one fitting the goals and ethos of the constructive view—should build on this long and worthy tradition of "worldmaking." It must include two elements, in particular.

First, it must be global in scope. This is not to deny the importance of national or regional struggles for reparations, including Caribbean nations' CARICOM Reparations Commission, reparations projects formed on the African continent, and demands from Indigenous groups who have collaborated across their nations to push for redress of grievances. But slavery, colonialism, and the political structure they produced are global phenomena, and we need a global theoretical perspective on what could (and does) unite these separate political projects.

Second, and perhaps less obvious, a politically serious reparations project must focus on climate change. The connection between climate crisis, slavery, and colonialism flows from distributions of wealth and vulnerability created by centuries of global politics and its ecological consequences, layered with more recent histories of pollution in the Global North and corporate fossil fuel interests. As climate impacts accelerate, we can expect their burdens to fall disproportionately on those who have been rendered most vulnerable through the accumulated weight of such histories. Our response to climate crisis thus deeply constrains the possibilities for justice.

THE HISTORICAL CONNECTIONS between the climate crisis and our present systems of injustice help explain why a just future depends on reparations. Before the rise of global racial empire, different regions of the globe evolved in a fair degree of ecological isolation: ecological connections were constrained by the size and scope of relatively local human economic trade. The newly formed global racial empire exploded in the 1500s and stretched that trade across the Atlantic, Indian, and Pacific Oceans, comprising what some scholars call the

"Columbian exchange": a historically unprecedented flow of plants, animals, and pathogens into environments that had never dealt with them before. The results were immediate and world-changing. The introduction of European pathogens alongside forms of colonial domination, especially the extensive slave trade in Indigenous populations, led to 56 million deaths in the Americas over the sixteenth century—so many that some scientists estimate that this "Great Dying" cooled the Earth. This was the first anthropogenic global climate event, setting the political stage for the Industrial Revolution. In addition to the unfathomable suffering and loss of life, this catastrophic depopulation of the Americas likely enabled the success of the European campaigns of imperial conquest.

When the Industrial Revolution followed centuries later, human production for the first time outpaced the natural constraints on growth. The British Empire, where this process started, was already dominating key parts of the world, including much of the Indian subcontinent. These regimes of exploitation coincided with a crucial bit of geological luck: England had more available coal on its islands than competitors in Europe or South Asia. British industrialists developed techniques to extract and use coal energy to compete with the Indian producers, which lead to new forms of iron production and thus mechanization, crucially in the textile industry that converted cotton from the U.S. South into clothing for the entire world. Coal-powered, mechanized production revolutionized British manufacturing and the economic world, helping to complete its dominance as a colonial power. And this aspect of the global racial empire—industrialism—would transform the ecological world.

Although coal was overtaken by oil after the 1950s, the use of oil, coal, and other fossil fuels since the onset of the Industrial Revolution has sent billions of tons of carbon dioxide and other greenhouse gases into the atmosphere. The ecological ramifications of these carbon emissions are tremendous. If present trends continue, an estimated one in three humans will—as soon as 2070—be pushed out of the climate niche that our species has inhabited for millennia. In the Global South, sea-level rise poses existential threat to the Pacific Islands, Bangladesh, and the Nile Delta, while drought and agricultural failure leave sub-Saharan Africa on a knife's edge.

To be sure, some aspects of the distribution of climate impacts are purely geographical. Whether or not a family is affected by a hurricane or sea-level rise, for example, depends on how close they live to the ocean. But what matters for our commitment to justice is how these ecological phenomena affect people's capabilities —the lives that they are or are not empowered to live. In some cases, these geographical variables are themselves deeply shaped by centuries of injustice rather than by personal choices. In other cases, differential distributions of wealth and power today will only exacerbate inequality in the future. Some people who retreat from a coastline will have access to money or credit to manage the financial costs of relocation, a passport or citizenship status that will widen their legal relocation options, and a social status that will make their new communities likely to welcome them. Many others will lack some or all of these advantages: they will be cash-poor and indebted, have a citizenship status that radically curtails their mobility, or a social status that draws stigma and violence.

These outcomes aren't purely geographical; they are shaped by our social and political arrangements.

We know that the costs and burdens of environmental catastrophe will be distributed in ways that echo the history of global racial empire because it is already happening. Researchers studying New York City have found that heatwave deaths and even the temperature itself were racially distributed: residents in areas with a larger proportion of white people were wealthier and benefited from the natural cooling of more vegetation as well as the artificial cooling of air conditioners. Meanwhile, what scientists call the "urban heat island effect" put inner-city residents at risk.

Climate crisis is also likely to lead to new social divisions between those advantaged enough to buy or coerce security from climate impacts and those who cannot. Researchers link recent violence between neighbors in Mali and Nigeria to resource conflicts exacerbated by climate-related desertification and other impacts. At a community, local, and national scale, we can expect police to protect the rich and socially well-positioned, often leaving vulnerable those on the business end of nightsticks or behind cell walls. We can also expect the balance of power between nation states and Indigenous communities to be shaped increasingly by forces of the same kind: the climate crisis is likely to shuffle increasing power and control into the hands of those in command of wealth, coercive force, or strategic resources.

Putting all this together, the lesson is clear: to understand how the climate crisis will interact with global racial empire's distribution of advantages and disadvantages, we need to explore the distribution of specifically *environmental* risk and vulnerability. Various contested economic theories suggest mechanisms for why vulnerabilities are high in the formerly colonized parts of the world, but the distribution of environmental risk and vulnerability can be explained simply in terms of patterns of accumulation.

Accumulation is the result of distribution over time. If you and I both save ten cents of every dollar we earn over our working lives, we will both end up with accumulated savings by the time we retire. At small scales, the elements of choice and responsibility matter: if we both make around the same amount of money from our jobs and have access to similarly consistent hours, then in the end the person with the most retirement funds will be the thriftiest or hardest working of the two of us. However, if I make minimum wage and you make seven figures a year, spending habits or willingness to tack on overtime shifts can never explain the difference between our retirement savings. The distribution of income in our working years, not our work habits, explains the different levels of accumulation we have when we retire. What we can do in our retirement age, how we are cared for, and what we leave to our heirs, likewise, are primarily determined by this distribution. The environmental risk and vulnerability facing countries and populations today emerges from several overlapping strands of political, cultural, and economic accumulation, which were largely set in motion generations ago.

In 2005 climate change researchers at the University of East Anglia created an index of eleven key indicators for vulnerability to climate change impacts: percentage of the population with access to sanitation, three measures of literacy rate (by different age groups and by gender), maternal mortality rate, typical caloric intake, civil liberties, political rights, government effectiveness, life expectancy at birth, and a measure of access to justice termed "voice and accountability."

Such measures of climate vulnerability are a useful tool for the constructive view of reparations: what matters about the economy are the actual lives people are empowered to lead. And the measures clearly reveal that the colonizing parts of the world are now much less vulnerable to climate change than the regions they colonized. The measures thus reflect a simple lesson about how yesterday's distribution affects tomorrow's reality: heightened vulnerability to the incoming aspects of climate change correlates directly with greater deprivation in the status quo. In short, the rich get richer and the poor get poorer. It is not that every aspect of today's global racial empire is rooted in the impacts of climate change—but every aspect of tomorrow's global racial empire will be. Climate change will redistribute social advantages in a way that compounds and locks in the distributional injustices we have inherited from history.

IN THE FACE of these links, what should be done? We don't have to agree on every aspect of the new world we are building to agree on ways to improve the justice of our current arrangements. At the same time, even in times of immense political opportunity, the possibilities for change are profoundly constrained by the balance of power we inherit from centuries past. As Frederick Douglass noted, "power concedes nothing without a demand." It is thus imperative to issue clear demands. Here are some places we might start.

1. Unconditional Cash Transfers

Contemporary demands for reparations have rightly kept focus on this tactic. In stark contrast to the byzantine social support systems that have come to characterize modern social democracies, social scientists are beginning to embrace "unconditional cash transfers" —simply giving people money directly. These kinds of transfers will intervene directly in the patterns of accumulation, one of our most adaptable forms of social advantages. It also avoids the problems with other welfare programs: the sprawling (and questionably efficacious) overhead, the paternalistic attempts to further shape people's incentives, and the "poverty traps" caused by aid withdrawal once a recipient crosses some threshold of income or welfare. Furthermore, the ethos of the unconditional cash transfer matches self-determination as a goal for reparations policies, which is part and parcel of the constructive view.

In their recent book *From Here to Equality: Reparations for Black Americans in the Twenty-First Century* (2020), economist William A. Darity, Jr., and folklorist–art consultant A. Kirsten Mullen endorse a strategy rooted in direct payments to African Americans descended from those enslaved in the United States, disbursed over time rather than all at once (to prevent inflation) and via trust funds and endowments. Moreover, it would be governed by a National Reparations Board that enlists its recipients in research about and decisions over the funds, further bolstering a commitment to an outcome of self-determination. Scholar and organizer Dorian Warren of the Economic Security Project has suggested that we adopt a strategy rooted in "targeted universalism" —a universal basic income for all, plus an additional amount for African Americans to account for the owed reparations. These proposals have been discussed in the context of U.S. politics, but others have suggested a global universal basic income, which could be weighted in the targeted way that Warren suggests. Both of these are exactly the kind of demands we should want to win.

2. Global Climate Funding

Cash transfers directly redistribute social advantages in a powerful way, but they do not directly redistribute disadvantages, including the vulnerability to environmental harm and the burden of climate policy.

The Climate Equity Reference Project is an effort-sharing framework that calculates "fair shares" of the global climate transition effort to individual countries based on their "responsibility" for global emissions and capacity to mobilize resources for reductions in greenhouse emissions given their economic and development needs. Across a variety of ways of calculating "fair share," poorer countries pledged emissions reductions that greatly exceed their share of climate work while rich counties pledged far less than their share. In fact, poor countries have pledged 50 percent more in reductions than rich countries.

Part of the reason that richer countries' reduction pledges lag behind their fair share is because achieving the needed scale of change in a reasonable time frame is technologically difficult.

Another approach would be for a richer country to bear the costs of reducing emissions where there are more opportunities for faster emissions reduction.

The Green Climate Fund, managed under the existing United Nations Framework on Climate Change, could facilitate such inter-country transfers and provide other support. The rich nations and associated institutions have pledged to raise $100 billion for developing nations' green development, a step in the right direction. However, Mariama Williams of the South Centre, an intergovernmental organization supported and staffed by developing countries, claims that this "does not even come close" to what is needed to make significant inroads into the climate crisis. Moreover, the rich countries have failed to follow through on their pledges; the fund stood at a fraction of its goal in early 2020. Both the funding target and the follow-through by richer countries must increase substantially.

Funding the technology to reduce emissions is crucial, but how do we pay for crises and impacts when they arrive? The United Nations and other intergovernmental organizations typically refer to crises—such as those stemming from natural disasters like hurricanes—as "loss and damage." The question of who should pay for the loss and damage of climate change raises familiar problems in distributive justice: Should rich countries pay because they are richer or because they have emitted more? We can add another: or because they've inherited more of the liabilities from global racial empire?

No matter how we settle this issue, today's mechanisms for loss and damage funding show us what to avoid. Beyond the problem of consistent underfunding, the substantial flow of loans to Third World countries in crisis saddles recipients with debt rather than relief. Debt jubilee could free up vast amounts of public spending in Third World countries that could be put toward increasing climate security. Failing that, debt relief for climate finance swaps could reverse this: converting sovereign debt into fuel for climate relief for Third World nations whose money is better spent on climate adaptation than debt service.

3. Torch the Tax Havens

Financing the proposals above will require revamping the financial system locally and globally to prevent elites from hiding and hoarding the world's wealth, and a crucial component of such a program must involve confronting "tax havens"—sites for the accumulation of wealth, often ill-gotten, which shield wealth holders from taxes. In his book *The Hidden Wealth of Nations: The Scourge of Tax Heavens* (2015), economist Gabriel Zucman estimates that at least $7.6 trillion of the world's wealth was held in these offshore accounts. This is surely a low-ball estimate, Zucman notes, since his calculation excludes wealth tied up in real assets (e.g., yachts, jewelry) and circulating in cash, where much of the wealth from drug and other illegal trades is stored. To understand the scale of this mammoth figure, consider that in 2019, the budget for United States' entire military apparatus—including the Department of Defense, all seventeen of its intelligence agencies, its war budget for operations in Iraq and Afghanistan, its nuclear weapons program, and veterans affairs expenses—was estimated at $1.25 trillion, less than a fifth of the value of the wealth horded in the world's tax havens.

While tax havens appear in both the Global North and South (Switzerland, Luxembourg, the Cayman Islands, Ireland, Panama), the overall effect of their distribution has worked out to impoverish Global South countries. Zucman estimates that at least 22 percent of Latin American wealth and 30 percent of African wealth is held off shore, representing tens of billions of dollars of lost tax revenue that could be put to the service of crucial green infrastructure development, just housing, or other pivotal worldbuilding uses. Heather Lowe, legal counsel for nonprofit think tank Global Finance Integrity, reminds: "For every country losing money illicitly, there is another country absorbing it. Illicit financial outflows are facilitated by financial opacity in tax havens and in Western economies like the United States." Implementing transparency measures to curtail tax haven secrecy and anonymous shell companies is crucial to curtailing illicit flows.

4. Divest–Invest, from Fossil Fuels to Communities

Fossil fuel divestment campaigns often aim to move capital from problematic fossil fuel corporations to more "climate responsible investments." On the view of climate justice developed here, green investments in Black and Indigenous communities *are* climate-responsible investments. We ought to think of fossil fuel companies like we think of police, as generators of insecurity, and make similar efforts to divert resources from them back into looted communities. The divest–invest framework in both of these divestment campaigns ought to aim for this same pattern of redistribution.

Some might be skeptical: divestment campaigns don't seem to work—until they do. When they reach a tipping point, they can have sudden and dramatic effects. Each institution that divests poses limited financial risks for investors, but each additional divesting corporation increases the difficult-to-quantify reputational risks that could trigger wide-scale (and more consequential) market movement. A group consisting of fewer than 10 percent of investors, according to simulations, could trigger a systemwide redistribution of social resources away from fossil fuels.

Social movements can also be "tipped" in this way. In 2014 youth runners went on hundred- and even thousand-mile runs, spreading news of an incoming pipeline by word of mouth. Hundreds, then thousands, answered the call and camped around the Standing Rock Indian Reservation to defend the Indigenous territory from the construction of the Dakota Access Pipeline being attempted by the U.S. Army Corps of Engineers. Standing Rock was one battle in a larger confrontation; similar campaigns were being waged at the same time and continue around the world now—from residents in Appalachia opposing Dominion Energy's pipelines through their communities to the Kenyan environmental activists mobilized against construction of a Chinese-financed coal-fired energy plant on the island of Lamu.

Anyone within a stone's throw of an institution that is invested in fossil fuels—a state or national government, a university, even a company—can start or join a divestment movement, or oppose the construction or expansion of environmentally and socially harmful production. You can also demand that the divested social resources be invested in and by Black, Indigenous, and other colonized communities.

5. Decide Together

A question that is equally pressing for grassroots struggle and the formal halls of power is how to debate, prioritize, and act on these and other proposals. In much of the world today, representative democracy is plagued by elite capture: the manipulation of public institutions and resources by the most advantaged and well-positioned, often to the detriment of everyone else. As if that's not bad enough, many of the approaches to combating this very kind of injustice, including valorization of and organizing around marginalized identities, are likewise vulnerable to elite capture.

A better alternative than reliance on representative institutions is to emphasize the distribution of power itself. Energy researcher Johanna Bozuwa provides a helpful example in her summary of the work of many activists and community organizations, which she calls "energy democracy." Community control over the generation, transportation, and distribution of energy would shift the incentives governing how those important social advantages—as well as the associated disadvantages, such as pollution—are controlled and managed. Publicly owned utilities are no radical pipedream, even in the United States: they already serve small cities like Hammond, Wisconsin, and big ones like Los Angeles and Nashville. But beyond public ownership of energy, protection from elite capture is key to the pursuit of climate justice. Community-level decision-making and control of public utilities must be the goal.

It is not enough to say that we should listen to the voices of marginalized peoples in making decisions and controlling climate initiatives. Each of us will have to decide, after all, which specific perspectives of many we want to support. We shouldn't expect that process to be easy or without controversy. Groups including Indigenous-led The Red Nation, Cooperation Jackson in predominantly Black Mississippi, and the Pan African Climate Justice Alliance have each issued carefully developed statements offering broad direction as to what climate justice looks like in action. But the devil is often in the details.

Identity issues further complicate an equally fundamental problem: the formal structures we have to work with are not well suited to respond to global problems. Environmental policy scholar Michael Méndez details how a policy proposal for California to purchase "carbon offsets" split Indigenous groups in Brazil, with representatives from larger groups with legally recognized land like the Yawanawa speaking in favor of the proposal, and representatives from forest communities like the Apurina and Jaminawa speaking against. Whatever decisions lawmakers make, none of these people, who live in Brazil, voted for the California legislators, and none of them are in a position to vote them out. As Méndez argues, we may need new "trans-local" ways of acting and thinking across largely different geographic and political contexts, ways that emphasize the importance of community-level decision-making and impacts.

SOME MIGHT WORRY about the scope of this constructive view of reparations. They might think that a global focus on reparations as "worldmaking," linked with international struggles against climate injustice, could distract from more specific campaigns. But it is no coincidence that the civil rights movement and the decolonization of more than a hundred nations all occurred simultaneously in the decades following World War II: each of these struggles made the others *more* likely to succeed, not less. Attempting to prevent rather than join up with other groups' efforts stems from understandable motivations but is ultimately self-defeating.

Others could worry about the content of a constructive reparations program rather than its scope: that such a way of thinking about reparations will distract us from bread-and-butter reparations demands, like direct transfers of money to individuals and families or reconciliation processes. But this worry is misguided. The constructive view is all-encompassing: it would unequivocally support cash transfers to African Americans, for example, and reforms to education to facilitate more honest teaching about the history of slavery and colonialism. The constructive view is not a replacement for these, but a particular understanding of what they aim to accomplish: changing our social environment for the better. This framework simply identifies opportunities for reconstruction that include and go beyond these, linking the important need for cash and memorials to equally important issues, from addressing the destructive role of prisons and pollutants to building food and energy systems that protect us all. And indeed, in a world increasingly ravaged by climate catastrophe, the time is long overdue to forge a political movement equal to the scope of that planetary challenge. The colonizers of the world have never been confused about the scale of their ambitions; it is time they met their match.

HEAT INDEX

fiction by Emma Dries

(Finalist for the 2021 Aura Estrada Short Story Contest)

THAT SUMMER—the summer of the air conditioner war and the stray cats—it was so hot, we could only have sex in the middle of the night or first thing in the morning. I would have preferred to throw the blinds open and go at it in the midday light, let the sun bake us, get off on that heady delirium. But there was a problem of logistics: Liam worked during the day, selling solar panels we could never afford to the rich out in the country. His clients, exempt from any electric restrictions, had gamified their energy use: they pushed those panels to their limits, heating outdoor pools and hooking up enormous seventy-two-inch flat-screens—those you could only get from China now, and only if you were willing to pay an exorbitant tariff. Flush with solar power, they were required by law to return any extra energy to the grid. There was never any extra—they used up every last bit.

When I worked, it was from home. For a while, I'd made my money transcribing short packages of audio material for public radio. Author interviews, album reviews—my transcriptions cast me as an expert in the books I didn't bother reading, the music I never listened to. Eventually, I was replaced by an AI script that did my job in a quarter of the time, for free. Now I mostly wrote marketing copy for dying brands that paid me a penny a word.

WE LIVED on the first floor of a row house in a relatively empty part of town near the old university. It was my apartment before it was ours. Most of the homes had gone into foreclosure years back, and so when I first moved in the block was fairly empty. Recently, some squatters had taken up residence, and every so often we woke in the night to the squeal of sirens, city police cleaning house. *Move along. Move along. You cannot stay here.* Never an indication of where people might go instead.

One evening in early July, I spent a few hours in the backyard, attempting triage on the wilted spinach in the elevated planters. I had stopped going to the farmers market because it depressed me: tiny, mottled, dehydrated stone fruit—seven dollars you didn't have for a single shriveled white nectarine you didn't want to eat; just three lonely, subsidized stalls, and nobody was making any money. My own attempts weren't much better: the lettuce had surrendered to the heat, bolted into high spindly stalks with bitter leaves. But the spinach had seemed, at least when I checked on it, maybe worth saving.

Liam and I had let the backyard go wild, mostly out of laziness. We joked that we were helping with *urban reforesting* though no trees had appeared—just waist-high weeds and poison ivy, twisting in and around a rusted-over charcoal grill from a tenant or three ago. A scrawny tortoiseshell cat stalked along the fence perimeter, batting at invisible prey. I drank three beers quickly, squatting down by the limp greens, scraping cabbage worms off the undersides of the leaves, ankles growing stiff then numb, and when I went back inside with the sense that I was fighting a losing battle, I realized I was drunk. A mosquito had hitched a ride; I swatted, and it left a streak of my own blood against my wrist.

It was barely nine, but I was exhausted. I went into the bedroom. Inside, along the far wall, the air conditioner was slotted smugly back in its place in the window. Liam must have done it before he left for work. The apartment was hot and muggy as ever, but I strode over and hauled the unit—all its hulking, inefficient heft—out of the window. I slotted the screen in quickly, turned on the fan, and crawled into bed.

Two hours later, I woke to a grunt of pain from Liam, stubbing his toe on the air conditioner. He followed it with a sigh, almost too soft to hear.

THAT SUMMER was the hottest summer on record since record-keeping began. It was true that each of the ten summers prior had been the hottest summer on record since record-keeping began, only to be bested by the summer that followed. But that summer journalists finally stopped pretending that record-smashing heat was news.

The weeks stretched on with little rain, humidity saturating the air. The wood swelled and warped. Doors and windows stuck, and we had to apply extra force to yank them open. We stuffed pillows in the freezer for an hour before bed; when we pulled them out, they stayed chilled for a luxurious fifteen minutes before reverting to damp, warm lumps. Water dripped out of the tap lukewarm, cloudy and smelling of sulfur. We patched all the screens and rinsed our trash can with bleach, but the flies still swarmed and multiplied. They were sluggish, though, as slow as mosquitos, and I could kill them with my bare hands. Most food we ate came out of a can.

Early in the summer, because I thought myself a realist, I'd told Liam the air conditioner was neutered, sitting there in the window when we weren't even allowed to turn it on. As for my realism, we argued about that too—Liam said I was not a realist, but a pessimist, that it was entirely possible one morning we would wake up to the news that the energy restrictions had been lifted and we could run the unit as much as we pleased.

For the energy restrictions to be lifted, we would need a surplus of energy, and it was not news to the neighborhood nor the city nor the county nor the state that we were running at a major deficit. But Liam ran on a surplus of optimism, and he wanted to leave the window unit in. I hated the way it looked. It was ancient; I was shocked it still worked. For the winter months when it hibernated in communal basement storage, I had scrawled on it in red Sharpie, "Please do not take!" tagging a smiley face onto the end in case the extra flourish made a thief reconsider. But no one stole it, and every morning when I rolled over and saw that doodle staring back at me, my anger spun out.

Dries

"Sorry," I croaked into the darkness now, a small concession that was easier than beginning the fight again. Liam said nothing. I was curled on my side, turned away, but I could feel his weight, could feel him sitting on the edge of the bed for a long time before lying down.

WE'D MET ONLINE, on an app. This embarrassed Liam and bored me; there were people who'd met on apps who had children in college now.

The origin story felt false, anyway. The story I always wanted to tell wasn't of our beginning—I'd had so many of those—but of the moment we began ignoring exit ramps and pushing on. It was a story I couldn't tell in mixed company, though, one I couldn't even really tell Liam in full. I mostly kept it for myself.

It happened like this.

One afternoon, Liam and I were having sex in my bed when the fitted sheet slipped off. We had been dating three months. Normally, I wouldn't have stopped him, but the week prior I'd spilled a glass of water and it had left a squiggly light amber outline on the upper right corner of the mattress. It looked like a urine stain. I promise it wasn't—I promise that there must have been a little something in my tap water leaving that stain, sediment or whatever, but of course any promise like that sounds like a lie. I wasn't sure what to do. I was obsessing about it, about whether to stop Liam and pull the sheet back over its edge, when he said, "Turn around."

"I can't finish that way." I was learning to be more vocal about asking for what I wanted.

"No," Liam said. "Not that—look."

I looked over my shoulder. Patrick was standing in the doorway, looking quizzical, bowlegged from years of running on concrete.

"It's just Patrick."

"It's weird how he's just staring."

Would Liam find this staring less strange if my dog were named something less human? What was stranger, Liam's discomfort over our voyeur or my nonchalance? Did he find it odd that I didn't find it odd? I pushed him off me and got up to nudge Patrick out of the room.

"Sorry, bud," I said, dropping a kiss on his gray muzzle and shutting the door. When I turned back around, Liam was looking at the stain.

I told him about the water. He laughed like he didn't believe me, but then he called me his "incontinent girlfriend," which was both relieving and troubling. Relieving, because whether or not he believed me was irrelevant—truth or lie, he'd somehow found the entire situation endearing. Troubling, because I realized Liam thought we were exclusive.

When I woke the next morning, he was out in the kitchen, under my sink with a wrench, unscrewing the pipes. All I could see were his grey tennis shoes and the neon laces he wore because sometimes, with strangers, direct eye contact made him nervous and he liked to draw their gazes down.

"You hate how heteronormative this is, I know," he said, a disembodied voice from under the sink, and I did, but when he reemerged and showed me the Q-tip coated in brown sediment, I forgave him.

Dries

As for the monogamy, I knew I probably wanted it, but out of habit I'd still been sleeping with one or two others, even while it became increasingly clear to me that Liam was not. After that morning, I met up with each of the others one final time—I like to know when things are ending—and then no more, and no one after.

I WAS TEN MINUTES into a walk—clothes already drenched in sweat— when I saw Ramona standing catty-corner to me across the street, leaning against a lamppost. I recognized her from the shock of pink hair emerging from the back of a baseball cap.

I could have easily avoided an interaction, and yet I crossed the street, diagonally no less. I vaguely recognized the pamphlets, but when Ramona turned to face me, the bright green CEAP button clipped to her T-shirt confirmed it.

"Shit, Ellie?"

We followed the script: It's been way too long. I swear you've gotten taller. Matt's at a hedge fund right now, for Christ's sake. Rebecca won a lottery and moved out to one of the sovereign islands, did you hear? How are you handling this heat?

Then, Ramona pointed to the pin. *Committee for the Ethical Abstention from Procreation*. She ran the regional chapter, she told me, and the organization was flourishing. She spoke about CEAP as if it were a novelty, but I knew all about it. Members regularly staked out my neighborhood on a hunt for converts, though this was the first time I'd seen Ramona.

"Do you have a partner?" Ramona asked, fitting her hand across the top of her visor for extra shade.

I nodded and told her about Liam. We had been together for four years, but I sometimes forgot the answer was yes, maybe because, until him, the answer had always been no.

"When are you two getting married?" Ramona asked. She spoke as if this were an inevitability, a thing she was expected to ask, but when I said, "I don't think we'll be doing that," she leaned in.

"Really?"

"No, we decided to usher in the apocalypse with good old-fashioned hedonism, instead." She didn't laugh.

"What about—"

"I'm not sure," I said, because I knew where this was going.

Ramona reached out, enclosed my limp wrist, and pressed a pamphlet into my palm. *"Be fruitful and increase in number; fill the Earth and subdue it."* Her eyes were closed, voice laced with warbled contempt. CEAP's specialty was their loud and vocal war with evangelical Christian groups, who grabbed their pitchforks, secretly thrilled to have a target for their next crusade—for what was life without children?

For both sides, it must have been nice to have something to do. I do remember when it seemed like all we did was march, as if only to feel that unfurling ball of energy that jolted your veins—but by then, by that summer, when I looked at the fight, it was like staring at the sun: blinding, lasting damage. It was easier to look away.

"Rule over the fish in the sea and the birds in the sky and over every living creature that moves on the ground," Ramona continued. She

opened her eyes. "But we tried all that. And look how much we fucked ourselves."

WALKING HOME, I turned the anecdote over in my mind, deciding how I might frame it all to Liam, whether I'd bring it up at all.

Inside, he was washing a cutting board, giddy. A client had given him some imported Gruyère as a thank you for a tricky installation. "We could eat it on crackers," he said. "They're stale, but they're crackers."

I threw my tote on the counter. The pamphlet slipped out, deciding for me, and I gestured in its general direction.

"A CEAP rep accosted me." I'd workshopped verbs the whole way back; this one seemed safest. "We actually went to college together."

Liam turned and lifted the pamphlet between two soapy fingers. "You should have just said you were barren."

"Didn't think I should get into it."

"So what'd you say?"

"I said it wasn't her business." I'd said nothing of the sort; in fact, I'd given Ramona my number, not even a fake one, watching as she programmed it into her phone and texted me to confirm.

He laid the pamphlet back down on the counter. "I'd like to revisit," he said. Behind him, a silverfish crawled up the oil-splattered cabinet.

"I'm not sure I'm ready."

"So Ramona was just a coincidence."

Look at what we're eating, I wanted to say. A few slices of cheese. Canned string beans, gussied up with half-rancid oil and red pepper flakes.

"It was just a weird encounter," I said instead. "You know I don't believe any of it."

But Liam's face betrayed the truth, which is that he'd never known anything less.

HE'D FIRST ASKED ME about it nearly a year prior. It was early fall, we were drinking beers on the back porch and the fact that I had a sweater on in and of itself felt revelatory. How much longer was my IUD good for, he wanted to know. Four or five years, I'd told him, but I'd have to double-check. Why?

"Have you ever thought about having it taken out?"

I picked at the label of my sweating bottle. "Not really."

"Would you?"

"Would I take it out?"

"Would you think about it?"

He never asked me for anything. "I'll think about it," I'd said.

WHAT BOTHERED ME the most—and I'd often tried to explain this to Liam, who always thought there were better things to be angry about—was that everyone who'd screwed us was dead. One death reported on NPR during that latest, hottest summer: an oil CEO who'd lied for years about the severity of a leak in the Gulf. He'd claimed tens of gallons a day, when the truth was tens of thousands, and there we were, decades later and the oil was still spewing out. Dark slicks of grease, choked seagulls; you couldn't even swim at Destin anymore. On the radio, the CEO was memorialized as a "robber baron of the twenty-first century." He was never prosecuted. Nothing he did was technically illegal.

We'd stopped going to therapy because our therapists felt as bad as we did and were getting worse at hiding it. After all, the warmth of solidarity is a brief reprieve, but sometimes it's more of a relief to be told you're crazy than sane. I clung to Liam as though I could absorb his optimism through osmosis. It never quite worked, but just being next to it sometimes helped.

WE HAD A WEEKLY standing dinner date with my sister, Carrie. Usually Liam came, but this week he was quiet, which meant he was upset. He got fussy about the little things when he was like this. Now it was the fermenting vegetables I'd moved while I cleaned. Too much direct sunlight by the window, he said, and threw out the jar. We decided, through unspoken agreement, that it was probably for the best if I went to dinner alone.

Carrie lived in one of the few new developments downtown—a steel eyesore amidst a ghost town of shuttered fast-casual restaurants and right next to a tent city that spilled out from the ground floor of an abandoned mall. Every town had a skid row now. The tents were mostly worn, patched plastic from long-gone big box stores. A few families had built crude metal frames and strung up tarps. The fire hydrant was perennially tapped, water arcing upward and drenching the sidewalk, evaporating into steam above the hot cracked concrete. Carrie told me I could come in through the freight entrance out back, approach from the south to avoid the tent city. I didn't bother changing my route, even though it would have saved me time.

A fingerprint got you in the front door. I was preapproved for entry the first time I ever came by; how they had my fingerprint, I didn't want to know. Inside, I took the elevator down from the lobby to where Carrie, who worked in pharmaceuticals, paid an extraordinary premium for her unit on -6. Cool, content, and pale down in her subterranean bunker. Hardly anyone could afford an apartment in the building, so it remained half vacant. I'd never seen another tenant. As I descended in the elevator, a million of me proliferating across the mirrors lining the walls, I thought about what was right outside, children stamping barefoot through warm dusty puddles formed by a fire hydrant's spray.

"They promise they're getting those daylight bulbs in here any day now," Carrie said when she opened the door, stepping aside to let me in. She said some version of that nearly every time I came by. Carrie had moved in three years ago, but the air still tasted vaguely of paint. False picture windows came preinstalled on each of the living room walls, but she thought they were tacky ("You can see the pixels!") so they were always turned off when I arrived. My reflection in those blank TVs was grey like a photo negative.

Dries

The apartment was monochrome—black leather sofa, white marble countertops, gray concrete floor. The only exception: in the living room, in the middle of a square of shag carpet was a ladybug-patterned blanket and Matilda, sprawled on her back under a spinning mobile of woodland creatures. She was jabbering quietly, an expression of deep concentration on her face. Matilda was a serious baby, born in a serious world.

I laid down on my stomach to inspect my niece. She ignored me, hands extending upward to grasp at the suspended mobile, forever out of reach.

"Do you ever worry about vitamin D?" I asked, looking up at Carrie. Matilda's bald head was papery and translucent, veins branching into streams under her thin skin.

Carrie rolled her eyes. "The Scandinavians have handled it fine for millennia," she said. "She'll be fine."

I told her about something I'd read once, years ago, about a common parenting practice in Stockholm. During the cold winter months, people would place their babies outdoors in strollers for a few hours around midday, so that they would absorb as much sunlight as possible. Carrie looked at me dryly.

"I'd give her heatstroke if I put her outside at midday. She gets plenty of sun."

"I wasn't suggesting you do that," I said, running my fingernails along the gentle rise of Matilda's belly. "It just reminded me, is all."

"Why didn't Liam come?" Carrie asked, sitting down and crossing her legs. She already knew about the IUD, so I told her about my run-in with Ramona.

"You think I should do it, right?" I asked.

"It's fine not to want one," Carrie said, lifting Matilda from the floor and handing her over to me. Matilda's socked feet kicked, restless and indignant. "Parenthood should be opt-in, not opt-out." For her, this was true: a vial still sat, half full, in her freezer, if she ever wanted to give her daughter a sibling.

I often turned away from toddlers on the street. When friends asked if I wanted to hold their baby or nephew or daughter, I demurred. "She's scared of them," Liam would say, only half joking, but his calculation was wrong: he thought I was resisting him, not myself. I couldn't let any of that want in range. Matilda was my cheat.

Matilda grasped my index finger in her small, plump fist and squeezed with intense focus. "Thank you," I said to the baby. "That feels really nice."

I LEFT EARLY so I could make it home by dusk. I was grateful to be back in my apartment, though I missed Carrie and Matilda almost immediately. Carrie never came over anymore; she said it was too hard to travel with Matilda. But I remembered the way she used to sweep in from the front porch, full of the complaints of the childless she'd probably call frivolous now: the heat, the long walk, the blisters blooming on her ankles where her sandal straps chafed. She always entered the apartment as if seeing it for the first time, and I would clock the distaste on her face as her gaze flickered around the room. I suspected she thought of Liam and me as animals, living above

Dries

ground. I tried to see it from Carrie's eyes: the broken appliances, the peeling paint on the walls, the large south-facing windows radiating brutal heat even with the blackout curtains half drawn. But I loved our apartment, its blemishes, its history.

Liam wasn't inside, but I found him out back, kneeling by the spinach.

"I think it's a lost cause," I said and he stood quickly. A tin clattered against the slats of the porch.

"What are you doing?" I asked at the same time as he asked, "What's a lost cause?"

"The spinach. It's not as hearty as us. Are you feeding the cats?" Someone was burning trash nearby; the air tasted like rotting meat.

"No," he said, though that was exactly what he was doing. "I'm just leaving them a little dinner." He just tapped a foot sheepishly against the deck.

I looked down. The tortoiseshell cat I'd seen the other night was licking furiously at the overturned can.

"They don't even care how close we are," Liam said with wonder.

"Maybe they aren't that feral."

"Or maybe they're really that hungry."

"I'm still thinking about it." I reached out, and Liam let me take his hand.

He shrugged. "I really don't mean to rush you. You should take the rest of the summer." But it was hard to say what that meant, when summer would end.

"I'm just jealous. You have this thing I admire so much, where if you want something enough, you can shut off all that noise that says no."

"How do you think we've lasted so long?" pairing the barb with a playful hip check, as if to pretend he wasn't serious.

THE NEXT WEEK, I walked three miles to the nearest clinic. Liam had not forced my hand. There had been no ultimatum, but still, I could see a version of a near future in which there was.

The clinic—which did not discriminate between those who wanted to bring life into the world and those who didn't—had no awning or sign. Unlisted, it had maybe another year left before its location was leaked online, but for now the block was empty, no protesters in sight.

I paused in front of the building. Flanking the path were two oak saplings, rising from dusty soil, each too young and thin to stand without stakes. I wasn't sure how old the saplings were, but one was a goner—I could tell from the scorched tips of its scalloped leaves. The sun was a hot iron, pressing into the nape of my neck. If the second sapling lived, it would be a decade before it provided any real shade.

When Carrie and I were still young, we'd taken a trip to the Adirondacks. Our mother brought us right after the National Parks Act was repealed and the Department of the Interior gutted. Loggers were coming for the old growth quickly; Teddy Roosevelt wept in his grave. I don't know what my mother had expected—maybe some sort of quiet communion with nature. But everyone else had flocked for the same thing. The mountains were full of hikers on a last hurrah, a few dogged protesters still picketing at trailheads. We didn't picket. We tried to enjoy the end.

We hiked out to see the white pines, centuries old by then and long gone by now, wider at their bases than my mother was tall. On our way back, we stepped off the trail to dip our swollen, aching feet in the stream. The waters were glacial, startlingly cold. When I waded out, I stepped on a nettle, and my mother had to carry me the rest of the way down the trail. I don't remember the pain very well, but I do remember the way my mother said, in that calm and distant way of hers, "It'll work itself out," as if it weren't my body that would be doing the repelling.

Standing outside the clinic, I noticed that its brick façade needed repointing. But other than the new saplings, little had changed since my last visit, when I'd had the small, flexible plastic "T" inserted, not so much slid but jammed inside of me, my body protesting, doing its very best to push out the foreign object. The doctor stressed, "It's fine, that Advil you took should do the trick," with a cold hand on my knee and a look in his eyes which told me that my pain wasn't real because he couldn't feel it, because he never would.

I didn't make it through the door; I didn't make it past the saplings. I would never be like Liam, for whom wanting was enough of a reason.

"LIAM," I said in bed that night, when the light was off. I'd taken the bus home, and he'd restrained himself to a single "How do you feel?"

and two ibuprofen deposited next to my plate at dinner. I hadn't had to lie really, at least not yet.

"Mm." He was in his own drowsy dusk, that liminal zone between waking and sleep that made me feel braver. But I did not want to know the truth of what he might choose over me.

Instead, I told him about the Stockholm babies. "We could go there in the winter. Walk through the suburbs, see those strollers all lined up at the ends of driveways."

"That's such a funny image."

"Babies in cute multicolored snowsuits in this perfect Scandinavian utopia, none of them crying." I saw the rhubarb-red cheeks, the frost-shined noses.

"Should we just go there and kidnap one instead?"

"If they're really cute, I might not be able to stop myself."

A soft silence; I thought maybe he'd fallen asleep. I counted four passes of the fan's oscillating breeze before he spoke again.

"Maybe then we could go see snow. The fjords. All that ice."

"Of course. We'd have to do that, too."

LIAM CONCEDED on the air conditioner, carrying it back down to basement storage for me. But he wouldn't give up on the cats. He kept putting out dishes for the emaciated strays, who waited until dusk to gobble up their meal. Because they were feral, they didn't seek any affection from him, only food. I watched them from the kitchen, their beady eyes slipping across the backyard, their dark slinking bodies going still at the sight or sound of any disturbance. The cats must have known that the food supply was precarious, for it took Liam many days of feeding them on a schedule before they began to return at any regular frequency, before they understood the pattern.

"I'll stop when there's another human mouth to feed," he said, and I wanted to bottle the glee in his voice. On nights I didn't take the food away, on nights I felt like playing a kind God, I watched those strays eat their food and imagined myself as them, rigid and distrustful, stealing hungry through the night.

The days slipped by and my lie was still there, but so was Liam, a center of mass, radiating heat next to me in bed. Sometimes I'd pull him close to me while he finished, just to catch that sliver of hope on his face. August bled into September and the mercury never dropped below ninety. The solstice came and went. Liam still fed the cats, and I stopped telling him not to. Sometimes, if he wasn't looking, I fed them too.

THE PROTAGONIST IN SOMEBODY ELSE'S MELODRAMA

Randall Horton

ROSIE LEE BELIEVED in customer service. She understood you gotta give to get. My grandmother gave credit on the dollar, got mean when need be, and wasn't shy about using the double-barreled .22 in the chifforobe. Then there were the rooms. Rooms men and women entered, some trying not to be seen, sneaking through the front and back doors; others not giving a damn, preferring to let everyone know they were getting laid by somebody else's main squeeze. I began pouring fifty-cent and dollar shots from the kitchen pantry by the age of eight. By ten I was changing bedsheets and emptying piss pots after Rosie Lee knocked on the door and yelled, "Time!"

I grew up in my grandmother's house in Birmingham, Alabama, mainly because my parents were schoolteachers and she, being without a nine-to-five, was the only person my mother trusted to watch her child. Over the years, from the time I was able to reason and observe, I noticed the assortment of characters who paraded through the house every day, some comical and some tragic, like

Bookie, who moved into my grandmother's house to take her former boyfriend Bluejay's place after his stroke left him sideways, dead as a doorknob, on her bed. It took two days to figure out that no one in the family liked Bookie—we thought he was successfully living off my grandmother's dime. Bookie rose every morning at five o'clock, filled the entire house with the rancid odor of Blue Magic shaving cream, and scraped his bald head with a butter knife. Then he put on Liberty denim overalls like he was going to work, except that was the problem: he didn't have a job.

By noon his lip dragged the floor like the tongue of a construction boot—worn, faded, and mummified from all the gin it had soaked up. By six Bookie was ignant and a natural fool.

Then there was Catbird, the person who gave me the name Skeeter, who religiously wore dark seersucker suits, white shirts, and felt hats. This small, lanky man possessed the uncanny ability to make the most serious situation humorous, like the times he got paid on a Friday and by Saturday morning his pants pockets drooped like rabbit ears while he swung in the doorway of my grandmother's bedroom, asking if he could get a fifty-cent shot on credit, his body resembling a damaged toothpick. Bent into a half-moon, he would rock back and forth, crooning, "Teach me how to swim, Rosie Lee; I can drown with the best of 'em."

Dot was totally different from Bookie and Catbird in that, first, she was a woman, and, second, she actually tried to be an ally to my grandmother instead of drinking up all the liquor.

A portly woman who wore knit pants so tight they looked like brushstrokes on her uneven body, Dot instilled the fear of God in some men and most women. On days when Bookie was too drunk and Grandma too tired and I was not around, Dot took the keys to the pantry where the liquor stayed locked and dispensed it as requested. Dot put the money under her large breast. Every time she dug to give somebody change, I wondered what it felt like to be a quarter under so much weight in her bra. Dot could also play the hell out of some spades.

Spades games were especially exciting after the jukebox man made his monthly rounds to bring new 45s and exhaust the music machine of its nickels, dimes, and quarters.

Men and women would allow this interloper, the color of bleached bones, into their personal space, which did not ordinarily include whiteness. The jukebox man was essential to their existence but as out of place as apples on a lemon tree. See, through music he determined the rhythm of their blues, the octave of voices in card games, or who became Jody on any given night. It would be years later when I learned "Jody" to be another name for a man sleeping with somebody else's woman. The jukebox man perpetually carried platters of Black gold, where artists like Aretha Franklin, James Brown, Bobby Blue Bland, B. B. King, and Little Johnny Taylor hid in the sleeveless jackets of his Pandora's box.

While the latest 45s spun, patrons enjoyed the music with head nods and dangling cigarettes, playing spades while their lips sucked on liquor from small white cups and cans or bottles of beer. One card game I remember went something like this: Isaac, a chocolate-skinned, bald-headed man with a raspy voice, slapped his leadoff card on the wafer-thin card table. It spun north by east, revealing a ten of hearts.

"You gotta brang ass to get ass," Sledge offered with a pull, flick, and release of a jack of hearts. Her occupation was digging fingers into women's scalps with Crown Royal Grease at Deluxe Beauty Shop one block down the street on Eighth Avenue.

Understanding the mandate given, Bookie drew from his third-grade education, throwing out a six of spades with no eye contact. He banged his fist on the table and yelled: "That's right! I dranks Johnny Walker Red. Sledge, get your money ready, darlin', and by the way, your old, wrinkled ass safe with me." Before ripples of laughter surrounded the room, Dot's forehead became glued to the ace of spades. Her neck rotated ninety degrees for the men to view while she hissed, "How 'bout kissing my natural Black ass, muthafucka. Get on up from here, nigga! Next!"

ALTHOUGH *BROWN V. BOARD OF EDUCATION* was decided in 1954, some schools and districts waited until the early 1970s to desegregate. In Birmingham, the Magic City, that glowing republic of southern oligarchy, compliance came in the waning hours of the fall of 1972.

My mother and I entered Gardendale Elementary as part of the social experiment in integration mandated by the Supreme Court, and I would soon come to find out what it meant to be Black. Before my entry into Gardendale, every time I pledged allegiance in a classroom, it had been with kids who looked like me, kids with whom I learned to high-five, dap up, and shoot marbles between shotgun houses as we meandered into our teenage years.

Toni Morrison took the position that something was lost in desegregation. The "lost" doesn't celebrate the division racism produces but what came out of that division: a way of going against the grain for the sake of the self's survival. Taking the Blackness forced upon you—the nigga that you became—and making it valuable, something to be studied, imitated, appropriated, and commodified within contemporary culture for the sake of modern art.

Me and the kids I once pledged allegiance with were being conditioned to blindly pledge loyalty to a system we hadn't begun to understand, nor had that system pledged allegiance to us.

There had been dynamite blasts, water hoses turned on the throngs, billy-club beatings, dog bites, hangings, insurrections, and violence right in our own city; and yet, we remained oblivious to the outer world of segregation, encapsulated in our own subsociety of a perceived otherness. Maybe if we kids had been aware, or if our parents had been more woke, we all would have revolted against this narrative, or at least questioned this insane allegiance to a society not yet fully committed to our best interest.

And yes, I would watch the old Westerns with my father, cheering for the cowboys to do the Indians dirty. Even outside playing with my friends between the shotgun houses in Smithfield, I strutted in full cowboy suit holding a six-shooter cap gun, thinking I could be the Lone Ranger, when actually all I could ever hope to be was Tonto, a sidekick.

What James Baldwin knew—and I didn't, but would soon find out—was that there always comes a terrifying moment in one's life, a moment that contextualizes race and from which there is no return.

You become the thing to be hunted and treated like an animal. The trauma is difficult to remember and retell.

Then it happened. The ball was up in the air, and Michael Hallmark, my new best white friend, had thrown the spiral perfectly. I was so fast I thought I would jump out of my P.F. Flyers, and they were laced real tight. I wanted to jump high but couldn't jump high enough because the ball was sailing too far for my fingertips to reach it. The ball hit a girl on her side. I went to pick the ball up. She kicked real hard. Called me "nigger." And I punched her in the mouth with my fist. Hard. Red appeared on her face. Red blood rolling down her white face. She started crying. I started laughing. I wanted to cry. She called me "nigger" and I hit her real hard and it felt damn good.

Let me be clear. Eunice Pearl Davis, now a Horton but daughter of Rosie Lee, was never a timeout or stand-in-the-corner type of mother.

My mother never hesitated to give teachers full authorization to paddle without parental consent when deemed necessary. I have no memory of how I arrived at the principal's office to wait for punishment —maybe it was the eerie silence surrounding the "event" because the teachers knew something I did not in terms of the history related to Black boys and white women in the South. The memory of what transpired after my arrival is clear: Eunice Pearl comes into the office and says to the principal standing over me, "Do not lay one hand on him." When I say never, I mean never ever did Eunice Pearl utter those words in regard to punishment. I knew then, in this racialized moment, my response to an action was bigger than the act. But Baldwin knew there would come a time, and that time had arrived.

Horton

It would take a few orbits around the sun for me to understand the enormous weight, the intensity of the primal scene that could've taken my life.

My father, who left work with the ghost of Emmett Till on his mind when he got the call from Gardendale Elementary that I had hit a white girl, would years later admit: he had to go.

Had to. He had to because I was in a place that didn't want me, that said "Hey, nigger" every day to discourage me from falling in love with their idea of beauty, their idea of truth, to never mistake Blackness for whiteness in terms of privilege. The principal wanted integration, was part of a movement in Birmingham for equal education and access, perhaps was a dreamer in believing that all men and women were created equal. In his dream he saw the need to protect this Black boy from a fate all too clear for Black boys who didn't stay in line. The principal called a meeting with my father and the girl's parents. The parents wanted blood or neck and were not at all happy their little girl got clocked in the mouth by a nigger, but neither was the Black boy happy at being called "nigger," so we sat with the conundrum.

In the end, the principal sided with his gut, the question being: What had I done wrong? My parents taught me not to hate. I did not call the girl trailer trash or any of the derogatory terms I would come to know as an adult. Perhaps the principal had no choice if this social experiment was going to have the opportunity to work. But what about the below-the-surface narrative (by those who often control the narrative) whispering in the parents' ears: You know, he can go missing, done happened before. Turn up in the Coosa River with his face eaten by catfish.

I will never know how close I came to being seen at sunup with my neck snapped in Kelly Ingram Park, hanging from a makeshift wooden cross.

I would go back to school the next day like nothing had happened, that big-ass elephant no one wanted to acknowledge in the room, still present and accounted for. The kids knew what happened. I knew what happened, yet not one of the adults wanted to talk about it openly. No one cared to ask me about the trauma of that moment, the fact that I hit a girl when all my life I had been told that was the one thing never to do.

After that incident, I didn't associate with the other kids in my class. I only wanted to get as far from that racial madness as humanly possible, because it became evident these people were incapable of being human. I never saw the girl again. Maybe her parents took her out of school, unhappy at how white folks cared about the fate of Black boys in Jefferson County. One thing I am almost certain of, and would love to confirm: the little white girl never called anyone a nigger again.

THE NEXT YEAR, sixth grade, I would stroll into an all-Black Catholic school planted directly in the hood, across the tracks in Titusville. Thank God.

There would be bonding over stacked heels and platforms, circular Afros and braided cornrows. We would drown each other in code-switching language, the way we said mane and gull, and we didn't run from our own skin; as a matter of fact, we ran into it headfirst. We were in a cocoon of Blackness, and whiteness had inverted to the other—they were the others now, and we called each other nigga, but it was love, learning early in life to take what is given and turn it into something valued. I'd left hell and returned to a mythological paradise, if only for a moment. And yet, society would not care about the scars, the racial wounds bandaged up—but would expect me to forgive those who knew damn well what they were doing.

Birmingham isn't a popular U.S. city for major novels or film productions. Usually, when a person hears Birmingham, they instantly think segregation, Bull Connor, water hoses, German shepherds biting little kids, the scourge of racism. That Black folk in this southern city have always been subjugated and relegated to an otherness from which there is no reconciliation.

Whenever I fly now from New York to Birmingham, I make it a point to rent a car and take the long way to my parents' house, first veering toward I-65 South from I-20 West, then getting off at Sixth Avenue, crossing the railroad tracks into Smithfield. I like to take in the old viridian shotgun houses still standing in neat rows.

These were scanty wooden structures that offered a straight shot from the front door to the back: open the door into the living room and the next room would be the bedroom, then the kitchen, then the bathroom, then out the back door into a yard with a clothesline pole. Most Black folk who worked in the steel plants rented these lodgings from slumlords such as Otey Real Estate. Segregation made Smithfield an all-Black community with a few Jewish grocery stores that catered to Black folk. My grandmother's house, which stood at 127 Eighth Avenue North, has long been torn down, and there is nothing left but the foundation of a building that was once one of the most famous juke joints in town.

The one thing Birmingham taught me—and perhaps herein lies my fascination with a city so complicated—is that I never questioned what it meant to be a Black American in the South.

Birmingham conditioned me in a way that has never left me feeling insecure about my pigmentation, why it does and doesn't matter. I've never been confused about this aspect of my reality. When I left Birmingham, I began to see other shades of Blackness and came to understand that there were many who grew up having to ask the question: Am I Black enough?

Growing up, no one in my immediate family ever taught me to look at the world through a white gaze as if it would be the secret formula to a prosperous and meaningful life. Blackness was always the center. My kindergarten was all Black, the first elementary school I attended was all Black, and so was the high school I graduated from in 1979. I went to all-Black summer camps, played on all-Black sports teams, never once questioning the idea of Black or Blackness.

People who did not grow up in Birmingham often disparagingly say they can't imagine how Black people can grow up there, let alone thrive, which I find interesting, given that every city I've lived in has been filled with racism, whether out in the open or hidden in an invisible dialogue that exposes itself most notably through economics and housing.

Whenever I tell people I was born and raised in Birmingham, I get a condescending look, as if to say, I'm sorry. I used to fall for this sentimentality, but nowadays, it is I who feel sorry for the sympathizers because they have been lulled into a trap. I live in New York City, one of the most literary and culturally diverse places in the country. And yet, I can walk out of my tenement on 136th Street and bear witness to racism and discrimination all day long. Just because you don't hear the word "nigger" doesn't mean a nigger doesn't exist within the eyes of people walking up and down your block.

I will admit that being culturally deprived harmed me, and it took years before I understood other people's idea of Blackness, or what it meant to come from the African diaspora. At one time I thought Birmingham Black was the only kind of Black; now I know better than to make this narrow assumption, yet I am shaped to this day by a sense of belonging to a particular region, in a particular time, to a particular set of circumstances. It is often said the idea of Blackness is an avant-garde phenomenon, a never-ending reconfiguration, a color adjusting to the contours of society while leaning toward another destination—an arrival and departure—always shape-shifting for the sake of self, for the sake of survival.

I am in the epilogue years and the path forward is not dictated by anyone but me. In the end, perhaps there is no escaping the history one was destined to create. We are historical beings.

Race matters, and there is no outrunning a lived reality. Every Black man is a protagonist in somebody else's melodrama. There is always a scene, a setting, a backstory. Today my life is compounded by the effects of racism and of having been incarcerated, yet I manage not to be a statistic, not to be stuck in an ever-present stasis, unable to free myself from the invisible clutches of a system that would chew me up and spit me out raw.

Maybe my diatribe is a lament. Maybe color will eat my Black ass alive. Maybe there are experiences I will live and die with and never understand. Maybe I will forever linger between arriving and departing, stuck in media res—always a-holding. Holding to hold on.

TWO POEMS

Adebe DeRango-Adem

(Winner of the 2021 Boston Review *Annual Poetry Contest)*

EDITORS' NOTE:

The lines of "Vox Genus / Provectus" recall the jazz-inflected voices of Black Arts luminaries. To say that Adebe DeRango-Adem is aware of working inside of a lineage is to draw attention to the unique musicality of her verse. The poem weaves together everything from contemplations on Ethiopia's colonial history to playful references to hip hop, all while serving the reader line after line of deeply memorable turns of phrase. We eagerly await more from DeRango-Adem.

VOX GENUS / PROVECTUS

THESE LINES BE A LONG TIME COMING / they come from
primordial scream   forecasts   varieties of false teeth   & a taste
for   self   the dark fascinating   rhythms   insurgent
throughout my genealogy /   a lingering auricular-oracular   line
       that begins   in a village   with a great-great
uncle who dealt in kinetic   currency / saw all through third eye
       & spoke   with an older   axumite   knowledge
       & my father before he was my father   belonged to a people who
had   names   for all the stars above hambaricho mountain / knew
their place   in the lineage   & were known to   frequent
frequencies   beyond   the small arc   of western suffering /
moved   as unburied marvels   & kept moving on
       missionaries   stepping outta line   & finally carved
       as though by magic   churches from underground   rock
          threw rome a bone   & called it a day   & when the
italians came again in 1896   they had slim picks & lost   trying
to decipher the spirit   on ethiop's lips   / so should
you wonder   what country I am   *reeeeeally* from   you
will have to play it way-*wicka-wicka-wicka*-wayyyyy back   to the age of
mystics &   wizards by trade   to come from my country
is to arrive at the beginning   of multitudes   these   pages
once upon a tree   but the rhizomes   beneath
       a   scattered   network   of   howls

DeRango-Adem

VOX CONSONE / NAVITAS

HEAR   ME   OUT   /   DEAR   BREAD   OF   LIFE
pantry on carnegie   ave / dear botanical   gardens   /
thing of curatorial beauty   I can try & tune   out   the
loud swirling   of trees / green as money   / that beautify the
broken   streets / try & drown   out   the   sound of
the vacant   rowhomes empty abodes / of dead millionaires
     with songs   on the radio / but when that song   about   the
rains   in africa   comes on / I begin   dreaming of axum
nubia / how we reigned   / in reality I am facing lake erie
     & the marina /   where two Black men in thick   camouflage
coats fish & talk   about God   / in reality they are likely
/ conversing in murmurs / grunts   in veteran speak / & by this time
it is raining   ever so   slightly   on   euclid /   &   I   pass
two more elderly   men / with soft branches   for a body
 / & in an abstract maternal   gesture / as if to say   sorry
for the war   that conscripted you   so as to script your life
/ into a theatre of pain

(or is it / the pain we share / I see /
in which I am / your understudy)

          / a production in which you are known for
          your famous last lines

(or do we need / to switch up
that storyline)

/ including the one that "philanthropy"
wasn't   the   result   of   "giving"
Black   people   hell

& still we gave

you   our children
who   became   your
mistresses

even gave you our   musics

let you mimic   our medicinal   blues

what   say   you   amiri
I   can   hear   you

sonia   hear   you   hughes

is it because we made you that you don't want us because
you
need us   like   sight

needs darkness   to   make   sense
of   light

DeRango-Adem

TWO POEMS
Maya Marshall

An Abortion Ban

is a body snatcher,
is an ethnic cleansing.

The uterus is a cave,
is an incubator, is a vault,

is a self-destructing bomb,
is a thoroughfare.

Semen is an innocent bystander.
Penises are just boys being.

A woman is a vestibule.

A judge is a strict father,
is Joseph awed by his father's creation,

is Joseph relieved of fault,
is Joseph saving face.

A woman is a support beam.
A girl is a receptacle.

A fetus without lungs is an unlucky horseshoe.
A fetus in a homeless woman is an empty pillowcase.

An embryo is a fingernail.
A fetus is a jail.

A woman who miscarries is a quarterback—
executed. Point blank.

A woman with a felony is insulation.
An angry man with a staircase is a felony-maker.

A livebirth with a dead mother is a school lunch.
A stillbirth is a twenty-thousand-dollar bill.

A pregnant black woman is a dead black woman.
A black woman who miscarries is a dead crow.

Marshall

A state legislature is a vulture.
A choice is a liability.

A Planned Parenthood is a desert.
A Planned Parenthood is an oasis.

A woman is a treasure chest.
A woman is a former voter.

A uterus is a leash.
A stillbirth is a tether.

A thirteen-year-old is a child. Only that.
A woman is a bloom.

A seed is an explosive.
Fertilizer is a shackle.

A woman is a target
A uterus is a target.
A felon is a target.

The Field of Blood

In the hospital, the man I love lowers
his eyes. Catheter. Cotton.
I join his mother for a walk.

If I were your mother,
I'd tell you not to marry him.
My own mother says

I can't stay with a sick man.
You want to fix everything.
Why should we leave good things broken?

*

On some night, my love says
I wouldn't want to be black. I—
I try to understand how he could

call blackness the burden,
not the whiteness heaped on top of it.
Blackness is not a failure

of the body. I bleed daily
for a month,
produce a liver-shaped thing.

Marshall

He rinses his blood
with a chemical cocktail
every third Thursday.
We make nothing—no child
no pacts—but distance,
until we both lose.

*

On some day, in our home,
my love says our child
would not be black.

But we're American,
I think, and say
she would.

*

He thinks we understand each
other because of his illness
and my blackness,

but my blackness
does not make me sick.
Love has betrayed my heart.

*

I'm sure Judas loved Jesus, but fear is a tyrant.
In this story, you're Judas and I'm Judas too.

A cynic would say he just loved money more.
But what would they say to the field of blood?

I loved my man and our cats but the girl in my chest
will always chase the storm in the field, abandon

the ghost in the house, leave the blood and water
running in the bathtub and hair on the floor, walk

into the warm spring night in a blackout, follow the moon
down the sidewalk—eyes glinting like the backyard cougars

of my youth—and leave you with your bare heart
and your mended bones waiting for me

to come back. A version of me will leave and let the felines
starve, because the beast in me does not want to be needed.

A cat's cry mimics an infant's cry.
I like to think I could deny even this.

Marshall

NEITHER CHAOS NOR QUEST: TOWARD A NONNARRATIVE MEDICINE

Brian Teare

THE CLINIC WAS OPEN once a week. It saw patients in a borrowed space near enough that I could walk to it, even on a bad day. Walking slow in my cognitive fog, only once did I have to pause, leaning over the curb, to vomit discreetly between parked cars. Nausea and migraine washed over most of that year. Since May I'd been enrolled in a taxpayer-funded, city-run public health program for uninsured, low-income residents who made too much income to qualify for Medicare. Late that spring, I'd taken the bus to my intake appointment with the health department; I'd provided the required proof—identity, residence, income—and I'd been enrolled; I'd immediately begun paying the modest income-adjusted quarterly fees, despite the fact that the soonest I could get an appointment was August.

Over the summer I'd continued to work as an adjunct professor and freelance book reviewer. During those months, my partner and I accumulated the hope that in August I'd at last get the help I needed. Despite temporary relief provided by weekly acupuncture treatments at a sliding-scale practice, my symptoms remained the same: occipital migraines, cognitive fog, facial flushing, nausea and bloating, and alternating diarrhea and constipation. I was always tired, always in need of more sleep; I could never get rested. My face and scalp were red and hot. Even brief touch left white prints on my swollen skin. The heat was painful and distracting. When I worked from home, I wore a big ice pack on top of my head while I graded papers or wrote. Curving around my face as it thawed, it made me look like a Puritan hausfrau, and my partner joked it was drag: the famous American poet Man Bradstreet. I took it off only long enough to freeze it again. My hands, however hot my face, were always cold.

The clinic carved its borrowed hours out of offices in a brutalist building of pebble-textured concrete and big glass windows, offices with dark tile floors that got colder as the season wore on. Its operations were obviously makeshift, from quickly taped-up, thinly laminated intake signs to shoddy xeroxes I was given on a chipped clipboard. Given my own precarity, I recognized a shoestring budget when I saw one, and I had sympathy for working under those conditions. When I finally saw the doctor—a pleasant enough middle-aged butch whose partner, I would find out, was looking for adjunct classes, and did I have any leads for her?—we had twenty minutes. Her back to me, she looked up my symptoms in a digital database. At the time, the facial flushing caused me the most immediate distress, so that's what she focused on. After cross-referencing her database, my family history of autoimmune disorders, my own history of celiac disease and osteoarthritis, and my litany of unexplained complaints, she found plausible causes in three diseases, and said that we'd do a series of tests: first for Sjögren's syndrome, then for lupus, and finally for carcinoid syndrome.

Then came the worst part: the doctor would have to order the equipment to perform the lab work, and was only allowed to order one test at a time. I'd have to come back the following week, when the kind and handsome phlebotomist, Jesse, would have one butterfly needle and one tube waiting for a good vein. I'd get the result the following month, at which point, if it was negative, she'd have to order another test and we'd start all over again. It was, at best, a farce, at worst, a bureaucratic allegory out of Kafka. While the doctor acknowledged the absurd, cruel inefficiency of the constrained clinic, she nonetheless remained its diligent and perfunctory functionary. Even when offering me a handshake at the end of the appointment, she remained behind her outdated desktop, a boxy model the same stained beige color as the public architecture from which the clinic cribbed its limited care.

And so we waited, my partner and I. We waited to hear the story about my body we thought Western medicine was going to tell us, the story of restitution that we'd been promised only it could tell, the familiar one that goes: illness, diagnosis, treatment, health. We also waited for my story about bad capitalism to end—exploitative labor, low income, chronic illness, and a health care system that at that time denied insurance to people with preexisting medical conditions—and for another, better story offered by taxpayer-funded public health care to begin.

As in a fairy tale, I was tested three times. The first time, we waited, I went back to the clinic, Jesse drew my blood, we waited, I went back to the clinic, and I did not have Sjögren's. The second time, we waited, I went back to the clinic, Jesse drew my blood, we waited, I went back to the clinic, and I did not have lupus. The final time, we waited, I went back to the clinic, Jesse drew my blood, we waited, I went back to the clinic, and I did not have carcinoid syndrome. In this way, months passed. It was December when the doctor told me I did not have carcinoid syndrome—an illness associated with advanced liver cancer—and because it was our final appointment together, she offered me a diagnosis—anxiety and depression—accompanied by two prescriptions, an anti-anxiety drug and an SSRI.

Though it would be another three years until I received adequate medical care, and though this would not be the worst I would receive, it was the first time I was betrayed by my own GP. She didn't say the phrase *It's all in your head*, but she might as well have. Given the historical mistreatment of women and queers who've entrusted body and mind to the clinic, I was especially galled to find a butch colluding with patriarchy's classic strategy of gaslighting. So much for queer solidarity! I was galled, and then I was angry.

That final appointment also happened to be the only one my partner was able to attend. We'd waited together through all three tests and there he finally was, listening to the doctor imply *It's all in your head*. I was angry because I could tell he wanted to believe her. I was angry because *of course* I was anxious. Since May, I'd been waiting to receive care. Since August, I'd been tested for a series of diseases that escalated in seriousness from debilitating to terminal. Since my blood was last drawn, we'd been living with the fear I had advanced cancer. All along, I was always already ill, dealing with the dailiness of that while teaching four adjunct classes at three different schools. She shook my hand and handed me the scripts she wished me to follow.

My partner walked out of the clinic and I followed into a disagreement that began the end of our marriage. We didn't even celebrate the news that I didn't have cancer. *I can't believe I'm with another crazy person*, he said, as though to himself, *Why am I always with a crazy person?* This only made me angrier. He implied that if I *did* have a psychiatric disability, I wasn't worthy of his love, that being with me would be a mistake.

I'm not crazy, I'm sick, is all the language I had just then. We'd been together for six years. I was too stunned to argue. This was my love, after all, the man who just that summer had helped me assess the limitations that had accrued during my illness. We sat at the kitchen table while I worried over an invitation to submit work to an anthology of disability poetry—*I don't really count as disabled, right?* I asked him. He was silent so long that I had my answer, even before he looked me in the eyes and listed the abilities I had lost in the years we had been together, physical and cognitive limitations that I had learned to live with. What choice did I have? But through his eyes I saw that my illness looked like disability, and I saw, too, how it had impacted him. Though we never settled on how best to talk about our divergent experiences of my illness, the conversation brought a new level of intimacy and trust between us.

How then could I make him see me again as a person whose word he could trust? The doctor's scripts were in my pocket; I knew I would never use them. In the coming year, I'd begin to suspect my love would never again take my side, and by the end of our marriage I'd realize that, indeed, he never did.

I'm not blaming chronically underfunded public health care for the marital problems created by exploitative labor, low income, chronic illness, and lack of health insurance. But neither am I absolving it of its part in exacerbating and complicating the preexisting conditions of capitalism. I keep imagining what it would have meant to have encountered a doctor who said, *I'm at the end of the care I can give you, and though I couldn't diagnose your illness, I believe you are ill and you need more comprehensive testing than public health can provide.* What would it have meant for my partner to hear *those* words at that crucial moment? I won't pretend that turning this experience into narrative is healing. The damage done to my life can't be undone.

If my life had been structured like a fairy tale, I would have been the protagonist abandoned once upon a time at the edge of the woods of illness, and, after I entered by a narrow path between thick dark pines, I would have been tested by experience. I would have been tested three times and each time prevailed over a figure of evil intent and the threat of mortal violence. I would have lived happily ever after. The fact that I lived to write this means that I did, in the sense that matters, prevail, but I didn't leave the woods of illness by dint of a simple heart and clear moral vision.

Fairy tales are known for their narrative expedience and relative brevity: all action is external, suspense is brief, and soon the mortal threat has been vanquished. But in the woods of illness, time stopped moving in a linear fashion, and the compass supplied by stories of the ordinary world no longer pointed north, pointed true.

Teare

The language of narrative—protagonist and antagonist, conflict and denouement—couldn't orient me in that landscape. No witch would perish in an oven of just revenge; no good woodsman would split the skin of the wicked wolf to find me inside. In the woods, all action turned internal, suspended in what seemed an eternal gloaming. In the woods, my sense of self became the unmoving atmosphere of the deep shade cast by the thousand thousand branches overhead. A thick carpet of dropped needles soaked up all sound save for distant wind high in the canopy. Cut off from the world outside, I might have thought I was dreaming, but I knew the sound my mind told itself was wind was really the unrelenting hum of chronic pain.

The woods of illness were wordless, though they burgeoned with sound, texture, sensation, atmosphere. The somatic experience of illness wasn't narrative: it was place. It was a place my body made out of its chronic disequilibrium, its migraines and nauseas, its gastrointestinal distress and joint pain. There was no story and no map, either. I didn't know how to bring anybody there.

IN ARTHUR W. FRANK'S FOUNDATIONAL TEXT for narrative medicine, *The Wounded Storyteller: Body, Illness, and Ethics* (1995), the ill, Frank suggests, need "to tell their stories, in order to construct new maps and new perceptions of their relationships to the world." Frank posits three common narrative structures for the experience of illness: restitution, chaos, and quest. In restitution narratives, the healthy person becomes sick and then they become healthy again, a quick, clean plot that reifies health in ways too naïve to be meaningful. This, of course, is the arc popular culture prefers.

In chaos narratives, the unlucky ill suffer without plot, their nonnarratives untouched by restitution or even just movement toward suffering in a more agentive way. Frank seems genuinely freaked out by so-called chaos. In his account, chaos strains the limits of caregiver empathy and institutional capacity because the chaotic body is nonnarrative—which, for Frank, is in effect to be a non-self, one who cannot effectively communicate or connect with others.

In quest narratives, the plot Frank prefers, the ill person finds the strength and agency to turn their experience of illness into allegory, a journey of insight gained from suffering. As opposed to the pro forma performances of restitution and the nonnarratives of chaos, quest narratives feature a "communicative body" that models for others that patients can "accept illness and seek to use it." So central is this narrative structure to Frank's conception of illness that he claims, "Becoming seriously ill is a call for stories."

Is it, though? What if serious illness doesn't or can't call for anything? Or if it can, it's only the body's call for the restoration of equilibrium?

Frank's view is implicitly Christian: it presumes bodily suffering has a higher purpose, and that redemptive meaning not only can but *should* be fashioned out of pain. His strong preference for reading illness as a quest shows that Frank's "wounded storyteller" is a *patient* in both the sense of "a person undergoing medical treatment" and of "enduring hardship without complaint." Dutch theologian Thomas à Kempis played off this same ambiguity in *De Imitatione Christi*

(1500) when he counseled readers to "studie to be patient in suffring." Christ was himself nothing if not a wounded storyteller, and Frank pressures the ill to make a minor miracle happen: to transfigure bodily pain into linguistic meaning that can be shared with others.

I find that pressure pretty sadistic, to be honest. Let's say you become seriously ill and seek medical care: What is it you're *really* called to do? You're busy dealing with symptoms on your way to see a doctor. You're trying not to shit your pants on the sidewalk, vomit on the bus, or migraine beneath the waiting room's unfriendly, unrelenting fluorescents. The whole time you're worried because you've taken time off work, you're losing wages, and you can barely afford the appointment, let alone what testing or treatment might come after. Your whole body hurts and you just want it to stop. Imagine what it feels like for some angel of medicinal meaning to show up just then and ask you to turn the situation into some fucking *quest*.

I admit to being unfair to Frank, whose chapter on what he calls "chaos narratives" allows: "The truth of the chaotic body is to reveal the hubris of other stories. Chaos stories show how quickly the props that other stories depend on can be kicked away." And if I seem to relish being unfair, it's because of the next sentence in that paragraph: "The limitation is that chaos is no way to live." No shit, Doctor Obvious! And though I will continue to be unfair to Frank and kick away his props, it's not for lack of gratitude that he, like other proponents of narrative medicine, insists that the longsuffering, uncomplaining *pacient* should finally speak. And I'm grateful too that he insists that doctors and caregivers must listen, even to so-called chaos narratives that "are hard to hear" because "the anxiety these stories provoke inhibits hearing." I remember well the doctors who found my language an irritant or inconvenient delay in diagnosis and treatment; I remember well the examination rooms in which very brief appointments played out with so little human contact they amounted to the barest pantomime of care; I remember well my lack of surprise when their diagnoses faltered upon treatments that did not work.

Though Frank's narrative medicine appears patient-centered, ultimately it underplays the fact that it's the medical–industrial complex and its caregiving archons who *allow* patients to speak and who *decide* whether to listen. Nothing ensures that they actually *can* listen, or will understand what they hear. Though narrative medicine encourages patient speech, trusting as it does that even the pain of serious illness can be transformed into language, when it listens it *insists* on hearing only a certain kind of narrative—even after acknowledging that the requisite authorial distance is often impossible for a patient with a "chaotic body" whose only story "is a non-self story."

Here we see the catch-22 of narrative medicine in the free market. On the one hand: "The need to honor chaos stories is both moral and clinical. . . . To deny a chaos story is to deny the person telling the story, and people who are being denied cannot be cared for." On the other hand: "Exercising responsibility requires a voice, and the chaotic body has no voice. . . . The chaotic body is disabled with re-spect to entering relationships of care." In other words, patients who can "pay" for care with narrative will receive treatment, while those who cannot "pay" will not receive adequate care despite the moral and clinical imperative not to deny them. The word *responsibility* is the dog whistle here; it calls up a classist and ableist neoliberalism that shifts the burden of "earning" and "deserving" adequate care onto the patient. It's an ideology that writes off poverty and illness as personal irresponsibility that "unfairly" burdens the caregiver and the system. Not only does this alleged irresponsibility result in so-called chaos for the patient, but it afflicts *the medical establishment with the anxiety of hearing about it*. After all, "the very poor and the very sick have only a marginal place in the case load of the professions," Frank writes, "which prefer what can be fixed."

The impoverished, the marginal, the uninsured, the unfixable—all of Western medicine's non-selves—do invariably, inevitably speak of their experiences, though too often they go unheard. And if their language creates discomfort, it is not because it is nonnarrative or irresponsible or chaotic, but because it requires a more generous and ethical interpretative framework than can be offered by the neoliberal clinic. In her landmark study *The Body in Pain* (1985), Elaine Scarry remarks, "Physical pain does not simply resist language but actively destroys it, bringing an immediate reversion to a state anterior to language." Because physical pain rends language, renders it in tatters, Scarry argues, "the success of the physician's work will often depend on the acuity with which he or she can hear the fragmentary language of pain, coax it into clarity, and interpret it." Scarry acknowledges the patient whose pain makes them incapable of narrative: what language such a patient might offer is necessarily fragmentary. In the situation Scarry imagines, it's not the patient who, through miraculous ingenuity and fortitude, transfigures their pain into story. Rather, it is the doctor or caregiver, who listens with acuity to what language the patient's able to offer and interprets it with nuance and care. In such a scene, nonsemantic experience is made meaningful, not only by the patient but through collaboration with the doctor or caregiver. It's no longer the patient's job not only to suffer but also to interpret that suffering adequately for others and thus "earn" their care.

The thing I resent about Frank—which I also resent about Christianity—is the pressure to suffer *correctly*, *meaningfully*, and *usefully*. One must strive to be the kind of patient rewarded with adequate care, the one who redeems bodily experience from itself. But in the context of neoliberalism, Frank's preference for the quest risks becoming a requirement, a form of responsibility-centered narrative medicine: the patient must not only suffer illness, they must also labor to make that suffering into a narrative with value commensurate with the care they must prove they deserve.

It's not that I didn't *want* to make narrative sense of my body during the years I lived in the woods of illness. It's why I ventured to the clinic; it's why three times I submitted to the doctor's tests; it's why I grew sadder each time I failed; it's why my love believed it was all in my head. Like him, I wanted Western medicine to give us a map of the woods. Indeed, I desperately wanted language I could follow like a trail out of my illness and into the ordinary world of stories. I wanted to be able to bring my love back with me and show him where I'd been living all this time. Instead, when asked to account for my situation, I would say, as is the custom, I had *fallen* ill. An easy shorthand as well as an implicitly Christian idiom, suggesting the realities of bodily life were bestowed on us by our fall from grace and expulsion from Eden.

But had I fallen as decisively as Eve and Adam? Hardly at fault by dint of sin, I could never pinpoint the moment I found myself on the path between the trees: one day, I looked up and saw nothing but branches. I found myself equally far away from everyone, loved ones and strangers alike. When I talked to my partner, I talked to him over the din of the wind far above my head; when I talked to the doctor, I talked to her through a screen of trees. What I wanted more than anything was for someone to join me in the woods: I craved a language of care as perfect as my mother's wordless hand rubbing my back when I had the croup and she bent me over a hot bath to inhale the steam that would ease my cough. I waited, but no one could come near; I waited and brooded over the way I had no narrative and no map; I waited until it seemed pointless to suffer also wanting to suffer correctly. I allowed myself only the suffering I could know: pain's rich and fragmentary language.

OVER TIME I REALIZED that, other than bodily disequilibrium, illness has no intrinsic meaning. It is neither moral nor metaphysical unless we wish it to be so. Like a koan offered to a Zen novice, illness reveals, more than anything, the desire to make meaning and the lengths to which we will go to make it.

Thus a meeting between a seriously ill patient and a doctor or caregiver is always a scene of reading: in the book of a fraught body, the text is pain. But if physical pain destroys language, and the ill patient can offer only fragments of that experience, then the text produced by physical pain, as Scarry would have it, resists conventional modes of literacy: "physical pain—unlike any other state of consciousness—has no referential content. It is not *of* or *for* anything." It's nonsemantic—it communicates no meaning—and what grammar it has is entirely somatic. How to articulate experience that remains physical?

This is another reason why I distrust Frank's evangelical faith in story: even if the social and personal contexts in which I experienced illness were relentlessly narrative, the somatic experience of illness was not. In the woods, nothing ever happened except pain, richly various, suggestive, yet endlessly repetitive. Sometimes, like at the kitchen table with my partner, narrative could briefly bring me out of pain's essential privacy—but try as I might, I couldn't find a way to bring anyone into it, no matter how far I ventured out into the ordinary world of stories. As Scarry notes, pain is an acutely anomalous state, and "comes unsharably into our midst as at once that which cannot be denied and that which cannot be confirmed," a situation perhaps made most poignant by the meeting between patient and doctor or caregiver, when so much depends upon language.

Frank's insistence that illness *must* be converted into story has always struck me as genre chauvinism, given that my own experience of illness was largely nonnarrative. Any attempt to convert what he reductively calls chaos into quest feels false, a wholesale betrayal of the somatic, nonsemantic experience of illness. And though I can't in good faith agree that serious illness itself is a call for story, I can concede that illness nonetheless contains a "complementary call for stories" in the need to tell "medical workers, health bureaucrats, employers, and work associates, family and friends" about the experience of illness. Indeed, the ill are so often asked to account for themselves that most of us eventually perfect the affected patter of an elevator pitch, a pithy account of a harrowing experience rendered less threatening: *I've fallen ill.*

But in what sense, and to what extent, can these stories crafted for the benefit of others be said to represent the experiences of illness and of pain? If physical pain renders language fragmentary and leaves narrative inadequate to the task of representation, then, as Scarry argues, "A great deal . . . is at stake in the attempt to invent linguistic structures that will reach and accommodate this area of experience normally so inaccessible to language."

Given what Scarry calls "the practical and ethical consequences" of expecting each ill person to possess the wherewithal and agency to become the protagonist of their own quest, I believe we must distinguish between a narrative that recounts the *social* experience of illness and a nonnarrative language that registers the *somatic* experience of pain. We must value them both, and in doing so, learn to read nonnarrative language produced by an ill patient, not as chaos, but as language made by a specific experience of physical pain and psychological distress situated in a specific socioeconomic context.

We must also reframe the meeting of patient and doctor or caregiver as a project of inventing, together, linguistic structures that don't predetermine the shape or meaning of a patient's experience. In the same way that it can feel devastating to have one's experience of chronic illness reduced to "chaos," it can feel unfairly punitive to *have* to refashion one's daily experience of physical pain into a quest. And certainly we must take the burden of interpretation and narrativization off of the ill and place it in the space shared between them and their caregivers.

I want to be clear: I'm not against narrative, which can indeed be useful, and in most medical situations is essentially compulsory. And I'm not against an ill patient narrating their own experience, which can be a complex and important gesture of agency over events whose ultimate meaning and sequence often remain elusive. The truth is that no genre is intrinsic to the experience of illness, and medical narrative can be a form of hegemony that ensures that illness is made meaningful only in ways that reify both Western medicine and capitalism as redemptive forces. It is for all these reasons that I make the case for nonnarrative medicine. I want us to acknowledge the somatic experience of serious illness, which doesn't take place in language, and when it does produce language, can be ambiguous and hard to interpret.

For a patient like myself who couldn't make narrative out of physical pain, it was easy to become disillusioned by Western medicine's structural inability to interpret nonnarrative language as anything but chaos. It was easy to become disillusioned by medical encounters constrained by neoliberal corporate capitalism, which measures care in efficiency and reduces patient–doctor contact to mere minutes. It was easy to become disillusioned by repeated encounters with doctors and caregivers who didn't have the time to listen to, let alone interpret, the nonnarrative language of chronic illness and pain, and whose diagnoses and treatments were thus doomed to failure.

And I was lucky. The doctor who misdiagnosed my chronic illness and pain as anxiety and depression damaged my life. But I survived to remember the useless prescriptions in my hand, how my partner walked out of the clinic ahead of me. I had to rush to catch up. It was cold and overcast, and the air felt good on my flushed face, hot this time with anger as well as illness. *Why am I always with a crazy person?* he asked, as though I wasn't there. Even then I thought back to the doctor's pronouncement with astonishment. She was basically donating her time to the clinic, I knew, and I respected that. But the public health program had an extremely restricted list of available tests, and there were no tests left for illnesses that fit my symptoms. We all knew that. How could she be so certain? How could he? It was a failure of care and caused irreparable harm. It was also the result of many powerful systems colluding to render my body chaotic and voiceless.

And still I insist my becoming ill was never a call to story. It was a call to restore my bodily equilibrium. And my anger is a call to imagine the clinic as a space where that could actually happen. I like to imagine it now as a site of contemplative listening, and the doctor this time gathering the fragmentary language I offer her. I like to imagine the doctor mindfully holding an odd cache of words that come to her in no certain order. I like to imagine her examining their nuances and inflections, their patterns and omissions. I like to imagine her very careful reading of the text of pain. I like to imagine now how it would have felt to have received this reading then, my partner beside me. I like to imagine how it could have shaped my subsequent care and my life outside the clinic. I like to imagine all the meaning we could not make together.

THE KINDNESS THIEF
fiction by Meredith Talusan

"MEDICINE IS I PERCENT SCIENCE, 99 percent bedside manner," Dr. Emma Larson-Donovan begins at the podium after she is introduced. Knowing sounds of agreement greet her from the black void of the auditorium, making it clear that most everyone there has seen the viral TED talk that launched her into celebrity.

Manila is the second-to-last stop on Emma's international speaking tour, which concludes in Jakarta tomorrow. Then she'll go to Bali where her parents have retired, and where her husband, Justin Donovan, will join her after he's done with his shoot in the Seychelles as the star of *Incredible Fury IV*. Emma's audiences tripled overnight when she and Justin married a year and a half ago, four months after they met at a gala for Doctors Without Borders.

"I have learned that the name of my hometown in Indonesia, Ambon, means 'drizzle' in your language," she says. "Now I understand why it always rained when I was a kid."

Emma congratulates herself when she hears chuckles. This is one of her cleverer lines, deployed in the slot for specifying the city she's in. She's memorized the rest of the speech she's given dozens of times as the world's foremost expert on bedside manner. Emma makes sure to shift her head every few sentences to mimic the manner of a spontaneous speaker while she explains terms like "differential care" and "data-driven compassion."

When her gaze turns to the side, Emma notices Dr. Panalo's face at the outer rim of the spotlight. Emma can't remember the woman's first name, but she's onstage in a chair, ready to moderate the Q&A afterward. Dr. Panalo hosts a local talk show, not Emma's first choice but her agency insisted the woman would draw the right crowd.

When they met in the green room before her talk, Emma guessed that Dr. Panalo must also be in her late thirties. They even look a bit alike, the same medium-brown skin and wide-set eyes, though Emma's jaw is more angular. Profiles of her often note that she commands attention, which is a polite way of saying that her features and manner are masculine enough that she gets taken seriously, but feminine enough to still be attractive.

"I read that your father is an anthropologist," Dr. Panalo said.

"He met my mother doing field research in Indonesia on the nature of conflict. I got interested in kindness because it's the opposite." Profiles of Emma dwell on this too, and how she lived all over the world as a child.

Emma is used to people finding this story charming. She didn't expect Dr. Panalo's mouth to turn downward, and for the doctor to still be wearing the same expression now, at the edge of the spotlight during

Emma's speech, an expression that suddenly conjures a young girl's face, the same downturned mouth from so long ago.

Dr. Panalo has grown up, but Emma must have known her as a ten-year-old girl named Liya, standing outside the hut of an elder named Tabayo, in a Philippine village called Pantubig. Liya carries a basin of water and the old man motions for her to enter the dark room where he is squatting on the ground with Emma, except that her name is not Emma but Manu, short for Emmanuel, and she is a boy. The village healer has determined that Manu will be his successor, even though Manu is only the old man's grandnephew and not his direct descendant, because none of his own grandsons are caring enough to be suitable. Liya is the one grandchild who wants to succeed him, but Tabayo refuses to choose a girl.

Manu has long admired the healer's work, the herbs he gathers and mixes into concoctions to cure ailments, the way his hands fix the villagers' aching joints so they can continue to harvest their fields. While the sundry store sells tablets and there's a doctor in town, the villagers still go to Tabayo because he accepts payment in rice and vegetables, and he's the only healer they've ever known.

"The medicine is not the most important part," Tabayo says as he lights a candle that brightens his eyes. "It is the telling of fortunes."

The healer drips wax into the basin, then peers into it with Manu.

"Ask them what shape they see, and no matter what they say, you must find the thread of hope that will connect you to your patient. This will guide you to the corner of their heart that will heal them."

Manu stares at the white blob of wax in the basin and sees a woman's profile, with hair past her shoulders and a delicate nose.

He looks up and sees that while Liya has left the room as the healer instructed, his cousin lingers just outside the door even when the sun is hot. Manu feels the weight of that girl giving up her place in the world so he can take his.

Emma can't help but peer at Liya's face now, which has grown longer and lost its chubbiness. Emma wonders how she could have ever thought Dr. Panalo a stranger, just because she must have married and changed their common last name, just as Emma has changed hers.

"The healing doesn't start when you treat the patient, but when you greet the patient," Emma says, though she feels no satisfaction when the audience laughs. She hears the healer's forgotten voice in her advice, dressed up like a minstrel for the Americans, then brought back to its place of origin at an exorbitant price.

Emma knew it once, that those words were borrowed, knew it for a few minutes when she wrote them in a book, before she repeated them in a talk. But there was no sense in attributing them to a person who neither read nor spoke English, only to invite questions about her past. To give the healer credit, Emma would need to explain that her father died in his sleep, that the anthropologist is really her stepfather who fell in love with her mother in a Philippine village before he came to Indonesia. People would wonder why she hid her true childhood in the first place.

Emma runs through more terms she's made up, like "halo of empathy" and "tactile placebo," recognizing how these are also versions of the healer's words, translated into English then medicalese. Though not just the old man's words, but his ideas, his thought processes, his entire worldview. Emma's whole line of research, the books, the money, the acclaim, were all stolen from this man and the generations of village wisdom he embodied.

"So if there's anything you can take from this talk," Emma concludes, "it is that maybe a kind hand on your patient's shoulder isn't such a bad thing." She hears how patronizing this is coming from an American doctor who has every treatment at her disposal, who makes dozens of times what doctors make in this country, for peddling ideas she stole from one of their own.

The audience claps.

Emma glances at Liya again, and comprehends that this woman can destroy her life.

She could apologize now, speak from the heart, tell part of the truth. Maybe Liya will take pity, and spare her the shame of revealing a past no one knows about except for those far-flung villagers she never expected to meet again. Except now, one of those villagers is about to interview her in public, the very girl whose rightful place she once usurped. Emma could pretend to faint, but it would only make the headline worse: "Movie Star's Wife Collapses Before Shocking Revelation: She Was Born a Man."

She needs to reach Justin; she needs to tell him before his team sees the news; it's her only chance before they go into damage control; he's on his shoot; he won't have his phone.

She's deluding herself. She'll have no chance once Liya opens her mouth.

Emma starts toward the seats at the middle of the stage as the lights go up. She looks past Liya toward the wings; maybe there's a stagehand who can turn off their lapel mics. There's no one there.

Maybe she can take the mic off herself, and ask her cousin to do the same. Maybe she can ask Liya to turn away from the audience, just for a moment, so Emma can plead with her. Maybe Liya will be merciful.

Her hand reaches for her collar to unclip the mic. But before she does, Emma sights Dr. Panalo in full light for the first time since the talk began. The woman hardly looks like Liya at all; her downturned expression is just the doctor's earnest face.

"Wasn't that fascinating everybody?" Dr. Panalo asks as she breaks into a wide smile, and the audience claps again. "Dr. Larson-Donovan, you honor our common ancestors with your presence among us."

"Please," she says before she sits down and crosses her legs, "call me Emma."

Dr. Panalo begins to ask questions Emma has answered before, about how she got started, why this research is so important to her, and even what it's like to be married to a movie star. She wants to say something other than what she's rehearsed, about a village that rests on the same land where they now sit, a healer named Tabayo, a girl named Liya and a boy named Manu. But she does not know how. Instead, she wonders if this will always be her fortune, to live a blessed life that isn't hers.

SMELL OF WINGS

Kim Hyesoon, translated from the Korean by Don Mee Choi

The therapist says,
Picture a bird in your mind
What kind of bird is it?

It's small and white
It's weightless and colorless, it seeps in and out of its white surroundings
It's lonely when it flies and anxious when it walks
I need to protect it but
I need to protect it yet
(The mumblings of a rescuer)
It has pink armpits
Milky white bird doesn't necessarily cry milky milky milky

They're all lies, really,
White bird who just chirped in front of me like a white handkerchief,
is bird that politely sips tea

When I scold it, bird says that it couldn't help itself
because of the attacks against me, the questions about my accountability for
my insanity, my violent language

Actually, I take up a lot of space
I'm about to become the grave of white bird
Every time bird says it couldn't help itself
I want to fly high up
but I get short of breath because my chest is too big
I feel as if I'll knock someone down when I spread my wings
So to be honest, I've never once spread my wings
Ah, ah, my wings are so big that I'm bird that can never be born

My wings smell like my womb's spit
stench of stinky bird

Behind me (What are you doing?)
the therapist says,
Now place the bird inside your breast and hug it

Next day
the therapist says,
Picture a bird in your mind
What kind of bird is it?

I'm bird that can be born anywhere
I can even be born through a sweat pore

Kim & Choi

No matter how transparent a bird, it's embarrassed when its body's too big
so mayflies are probably the least embarrassed among those that fly

Behind me (What are you thinking?)
the therapist says,

Now hug the mayfly

.

THREE POEMS

Savonna Johnson

some artist aesthetics to   travel pain into beauty   which vehicle in the taking   if
by truck   to haul   so   every poem about him   yes   then   there might be a breaking of
the heart   cliche   instead we must use   spacing   to tear one thing apart / to piece
together art   as if   a knitting has occurred   what one means by therapy   to
heal by herb   or   to vent   this is about the day to day   if   I want to ask questions   by
the different play-phrasing   *if one positioning her lips should*   not be able to say   then
with the collage   let it appear   this is the sexualization of [d]anger and
everything that might hurt   here   is this chamomile cup

there's dust every
where in this city i
sit on yr porch
pickin some
out my eye

there's that man
he stares in
yr half-taped-over
window be seein
yr goods more
than mine

4:30 in the am
you get me up to
get it in then
leave for work

i stay up after
to breathe
the morning

there's dust every
where in this city
you ain't got
no hot water and
i can smell my

Johnson

deodorant clumpin
feel the grease slippin
round the curves of
my face

eventually
i'll hop on a bus
sleep in my own bed
call bout gettin my
doorbell fixed

there's dust
everywhere in this city i
stay pickin some
out my eye

name your abuser:

call him a nice redneck New York accent, brake fluid, welder, call him the 8th of January,
a day before the hunger moon was full, call him a rented residential two car garage grease
shop, your neighborhood mechanic, call him problem child, younger brother, crack baby,
call him 6 years older and always right, tell them he attacked you with a white mallet
hammer and came over later that night to hang blinds

DEAR MOTHERS, WE ARE NO LONGER LOST

fiction by Yiru Zhang

(Winner of the 2021 Aura Estrada Short Story Contest)

EDITOR'S NOTE:

"Dear Mothers, We Are No Longer Lost" is a wondrous and beautiful short story about two people and what pulls them together and rips them apart. Intimate and atmospheric, I knew by page one that I was reading a unique and special voice. I felt held by such graceful and powerful lines as: "We Chinese girls were forever haunted by our Chinese mothers. No matter where we were heading in life, their shadows would always follow us, weeping like a lost child." Or: "Back then we could only afford to share a basement. It was poverty that brought us together, I often thought. In the soil of poverty, our love grew." This short story addresses those universal themes of love, belonging, and the desire for the freedom to be who we truly are. This is a writer to watch, a voice I want to read again and again.

—Kali Fajardo-Anstine, 2021 Aura Estrada Short Story Contest judge

MY GIRLFRIEND HAD A BOYISH HAIRSTYLE, the kind that you would see on K-pop stars. A bowl cut. A rounded shape with bangs that brushed her eyes. Sometimes, when her bangs grew longer, her eyes would hide behind her hair.

She loved her eyes to be covered. When I rubbed her hair trying to peek at her forehead at night, she'd push me away.

Her mother, who had immigrated to Montreal seven years ago, asked her to grow her hair because that wasn't the correct hairstyle for a woman.

We Chinese girls were forever haunted by our Chinese mothers. No matter where we were heading in life, their shadows would always follow us, weeping like a lost child.

AT NIGHT, I'd touch her ears. In the darkness, I'd gently rub her black earrings and imagine how the cold, silver needle penetrated her ear—it disappeared from one side, went through her pink, warm flesh, then appeared again at the other side. I'd imagine her blood oozing.

She never took her black earrings off, just like she never took her sports bra off even when she slept.

AT FIRST, we were roommates. In the basement on Rue Allard, we used a screen to separate the only bedroom. We put a single bed on each side of the bedroom. When the room was quiet, I could hear her breathing on the other side.

Back then we could only afford to share a basement. It was poverty that brought us together, I often thought. In the soil of poverty, our love grew.

"Why did you immigrate here?" I asked her when we first became roommates.

"My mother wanted a richer life," she said, "and she believed that, in Canada, she could achieve that life."

ONE EVENING, before she had become my girlfriend, I asked her if she wanted a massage. We were lying on the couch in our basement. Before she could respond, I put my fingers on her shoulders. I told her that when I was in college in Shanghai, my roommates would take turns massaging each other.

I prayed, when I was touching her spine, that she would turn back.

"It's my turn to give you a massage now," she said.

"You don't have to," I said.

Her fingers were cold. My neck was sticky. I was so afraid that my sweat would disgust her that I asked her to stop.

YOU MAY ALREADY SEE that my girlfriend was more like a boyfriend to me, but please excuse me that I'll continue to call her my girlfriend. That's how things were in China—if you were born as a she, then you were a she forever.

Zhang

I guessed that too caused her confusion, but I never asked her. It was something too awkward to be discussed. How could you ask your girlfriend if she considered herself to be a man or a woman? How could you just ask?

At home, I called her *baby*. I called her *dear*. I called her *lao gong*, meaning *husband* in Chinese.

When I introduced her to my friends, I called her *my girlfriend*.

In the shopping mall, she used women's restrooms.

In the women's fitting room, she tried on men's clothes.

IN THE SUMMER, she'd spend the whole night skateboarding on the streets.

"Try it," she said.

"No," I said.

"Just step on it."

She gave me her hand. I grabbed hers tightly. When I stepped on her skateboard, she began to run.

I bent down on her skateboard. Off we went, speeding down the empty streets of Montreal as the summer wind blew horizontally.

SHE USED TO WORK for Imperial Oil in Alberta, she told me. It was cold there; so cold that she dated her ex-boss. Their relationship started when their truck was stuck in the snow. It ended because they were both busy.

"My ex-boss is a white woman older than me," she said. "I like women older than me."

I was four years older than her.

"Have you dated any women before?" she asked.

"No," I told her, "I am not a lesbian."

Loving her did not mean that I was a lesbian, I often told her. Loving her only meant loving her.

MY SHANGHAINESE MOTHER's wisdom of life is that a man should be stronger in all ways than his woman. He must be older, taller, and richer. He must be mature, while his woman should remain a girl who never grows old.

My girlfriend was younger, poorer, and shorter than me. She was once mistaken by the police in Montreal as a boy under the age of twelve. When she went to Root's, she could only buy boys' shorts, and when we hugged, I often worried that I'd hurt her feelings by being taller.

In China, we described a lovely girl as someone who is "as dependent as a little bird," and a responsible man as "the pillar of a family."

In Montreal, after I found a job as an accountant in Chinatown, I started to give her money.

AT MONK STATION, I passed the entry gate, then gave my monthly pass to her. She waited for ten minutes to use my pass again.

Zhang

We went downstairs, passing by the sculpture *Pic et Pelle*. It was large, looming like a giant, metal spider. *Pic et Pelle*, I tried to say it in the right way. *Pic et Pelle*.

In Montreal, we always failed to speak and understand French. It made life even harder. But still, we chose here as our destination, because Quebec was the easiest place to immigrate to in the whole country.

On the train, we listened to and repeated how the stations were pronounced. *De l'Église. Charlevoix. Lionel-Groulx.*

The train stopped suddenly. We were asked to get off because someone had jumped onto the track.

WE BET WHO WOULD BE the first one to come out to our Chinese mothers. She said that she would. But whenever she mentioned queers, her mother would frown.

"Canada is a good country in every way," her mother always said, "except for the boys who don't look like boys, the girls who don't look like girls, and the smell of weed."

SHE SOMETIMES MOCKED ME for being timid, but she was the one who never confessed. She said that her mother loved her so much that she didn't want to break her mother's heart.

Her mother had always wanted a boy.

Before giving birth to her at the age of thirty-nine, her mother had suffered from a miscarriage three times.

After she was born, an intrauterine device was put into her mother's womb to prevent pregnancy.

Now, her mother said that she'd better change her hairstyle, wear a dress, and get married to a man as soon as she could.

THE ONLY THING that she liked about Montreal, she told me, was that Leonard Cohen once lived there.

She took me to Parc du Portugal from which we could see the triplex where he used to live. On Vaillières Street, under the windows of the triplex, there were tourists taking pictures, singing "Hallelujah." She took me to St-Viateur for his favorite bagels. In Mile End, we saw crowds cheering for France's national football team.

On a hot afternoon in July, we went to Shaar Hashomayim Cemetery. It took us two hours wandering in the woods of Mont Royale to find the cemetery, and then another two to find his grave. I finally cried because I was so exhausted.

I TURNED OUT to be the stronger, braver one. During a phone call, I told my mother about her.

"Oh," my mother said, "it's OK."

Zhang

"I'm sorry," I said.

"It's OK," my Shanghainese mother said. "Your mother is open-minded. It's OK if you like a girl. Is your girlfriend also from Shanghai? Remember, you must marry a Shanghainese who can support the family while you are raising your kids."

SOMETIMES WE'D FIGHT over trivial things, like she'd play video games at 3 a.m. and wake me up when I needed to go to work the next morning, or when I returned home, I'd find her sleeping on the couch, the dishes from the previous day still piled up in the sink and smelling like rotten eggs.

On our first anniversary, I bought her a keyboard that glowed in the dark.

On our second anniversary, I yanked out her computer's cables at midnight because the sound of her typing on the glow-in-the-dark keyboard was disturbing.

BACK IN SHANGHAI, I lived in a three-story house with my family. Thirteen families lived in the house, my family occupying only one of the bedrooms. At dusk, we'd wait for hours to use the shared kitchen. When we went to bed, we could hear every conversation happening in the thirteen families.

My mother told me that a woman's best dowry was her virginity. She told me that my virginity was the only thing that could change our fate and that I could get anything I wanted with it. She called women who slept with men before marriage *secondhand houses*, and those who had an abortion *haunted houses where there were dead people*.

I was confused about my virginity. I wasn't sure if I was still a *new house* after sleeping with my girlfriend.

WE USED TO DREAM about our honeymoon. We would take U.S. Route 89 from Canada all the way to Mexico, passing through Montana, Wyoming, Idaho, Utah, and Arizona. On the road, we would see moose crossing the willow forests, rattlesnakes resting on rock piles, and bison grazing on the plains as far as the horizon. We would kiss every time we encountered an animal.

Together in our little dark basement, we dreamed.

THREE MONTHS AFTER my coming out, my mother arranged a husband for me. Thirty-two, born and still living in Shanghai, owner of four apartments. He was willing to move to Canada to become the spouse of a permanent Canadian resident.

"It's a good deal," my mother commented. "He can buy you a house in Montreal. You can give him a PR card. If you marry him, then your marriage is a good deal."

Zhang

EVERY SATURDAY, my girlfriend and I would meet with our Chinese acquaintances in Montreal. We would play the Werewolves of Miller's Hollow for the whole evening.

I used to ask her whom she'd most like to be in the board game: the werewolves who do the killing, the witch who saves people from being killed, or one of the characters who might get killed.

"The werewolf," she answered. "I love pretending to be innocent. You?"

"The fortuneteller," I said, "who sees everyone's fate before they are aware."

I didn't tell her that I really only wanted to be the player chosen by the Cupid. In the game, if the Cupid makes two players fall in love, then one must die when the other dies.

MY GIRLFRIEND was always dreaming of being a real man. A real man offering his shoulder to his girl when she cried. A real man rich enough to buy anything his girl wanted. A real man who used male condoms rather than finger condoms.

"All of you, you only want to marry money," she said once when we were having another quarrel.

"Who are you talking about?" I asked.

"All of you. All the Chinese women."

I slammed the door and left.

BACK IN SHANGHAI, even if the three of us lived in one bedroom, we still managed to maintain our decency. Every morning, my father would put on a suit, comb his hair with hair oil, and wear cologne while my mother would match her blouse with her hairband. We would wear a different fake collar every day to pretend that we had different shirts.

My girlfriend never washed her jeans. They were raw denim, she told me, and washing wasn't good for the fabric.

ON MY THIRTIETH BIRTHDAY, her gift was a homemade meal.

"I wanted poutine," I said.

"My cooking is better than poutine," she said.

After she finished cooking, I refused to eat.

"Are you kidding me?" she said. "What do you want?"

"I wanted poutine."

I didn't want poutine. I was just tired of returning home every day and cooking and doing the dishes and maybe going to the grocery store to see what's on sale again.

MY MOTHER SAID that I would be a good daughter if I obeyed the arranged marriage. I did become a good daughter. Three months after the Shanghainese man's marriage proposal, he became my fiancé.

My fiancé bought an apartment close to the Saint Lawrence River. From the kitchen window, I could see the Ferris wheel by the old harbor. I used to dream about taking my girlfriend on the wheel and shouting out our names when our cabin reached the highest point.

I remembered those years we spent in that basement on Rue Allard. I remembered the roaches crawling on the ceiling, the sink filled with unclean dishes, and the pedestrian's footsteps that we heard in the early morning.

I BEGGED HER to come back after I was engaged. Getting married to a man didn't mean that I would stop loving her, I told her. It's just to make my mother satisfied.

She came back to me. She was lonely, I guess, without me.

AFTER my fiancé landed, I still went out with her. We'd go to the casino and lose all our savings. We'd go back with our hearts empty.

When I first told him that I would be spending the night at a friend's place, he asked, "Is your friend a man or a woman?"

"A woman. She's my best friend here," I told him.

He permitted me to leave.

EVEN if we went to the Pride Parade on August 15, we were never one of them. Those colorful, dancing people. Those who were proud of who they were.

We would never be one of them.

SHE TOOK ME to McGill's Redpath Museum. Under the dinosaur skeleton, she told me that she'd decided to leave Montreal.

One of the reasons I loved her was that she had been a graduate student at McGill. She was smarter than me, and smarter than my fiancé. I used to love listening to her talk about her thesis. All these terms that I couldn't understand. Richter scale. Seismic waves. Magma movement.

In the museum, she said that Canada could never be her country.

We walked out of the museum. Behind the museum, Mont Royale looked sacred like an angel.

DID I BELONG HERE? Was I ever a part of this place?

In the country where I was born, women were often praised for being thin, pale, and immature. A white complexion is powerful enough to hide seven faults, my mother told me.

Whenever it was sunny in Montreal, I'd walk under a dark umbrella. Sometimes, I'd wear sunscreen in the basement on Rue Allard.

"YOUR FRIEND is strange," my fiancé said after seeing my girlfriend. "She looks like a man."

"Would you believe it if I told you she's a lesbian?"

"Come on," he laughed and hugged me. "There are no real lesbians. They're playing make-believe. They are just lonely women who lack cock for too long. If they ever taste the sweetness of a cock, they will love it."

AFTER LIVING IN CANADA for seven years, my girlfriend decided to go back to our home country. Her mother refused to go with her to the Montreal airport on the day she left.

She told me that she always let her mother down. Her appearance. Her abandonment of Canadian residency. Her refusal to date a man. Her very existence.

"I should have been like you," she said to me. "You never let anyone down."

IN CHINA, cooperative marriages between queers are common to satisfy parents. Sometimes they even have babies.

Six months after she left, I learned from a post on WeChat that she had married.

At a glance I could tell that her husband was gay.

I wonder what their marriage is like. Is her husband's mother as loving as her mother, and my mother, and all these other Chinese mothers?

In the picture she posted, she is wearing a white lace dress, her black earrings shining like the roaches we used to chase in the basement on Rue Allard.

TWO POEMS

Simone Person

(Winner of the 2021 Boston Review *Annual Poetry Contest)*

EDITORS' NOTE:

"In Praise of the Sharp Blade" lets us see Gentileschi's famous painting as if for the first time. What better indicator is there of a great work of ekphrasis? Its gore-soaked lines invite readers to revel in the life-altering, almost sensual pleasure that revenge can offer. The power of the poem to transport owes, in part, to its deeply unmooring use of language: novel phrases such as "hunger-headed" and "crueled into rampage" are unforgettable. We hope Person continues to share her words with us.

In Praise of the Sharp Blade

After Artemisia Gentileschi's Judith Slaying Holofernes

or rather, in praise of the blade. its strength doesn't matter, we're hunger-headed all the same.
our fingers wrestle his cheek's crisp flesh to the bed,

a cheek previously motherkissed or held

by some moon-eyed love, and we pulp it into our good foundation. the hem of his neck stains
to flagrant soak, and we dig deeper. his eyes wildly bruising the room, hoping for someone
to gut us away from our will, but we'll tell you this: we, too, were once pitchforked under god-
swept wanting, and no one came for us, as none will for him now. we've no pleasure in this
frenzy—he crueled us into rampage.

o, blade, thank you for your famine of questioning. steady
in our practiced violence. how just it is to unmake a man.

Person

Cry Wolf

After Jean-Léon Gérôme's Truth Coming from the Well Armed with Her Whip to Chastise Mankind

I've strengthened my grip, gospeled my mouth into deathless cavity. I purged all my tender, and it's your name I'm hellhounding.

down in the well, I took my time. taught myself to sugar into cloying and knife under your gums. vengeance-electric, I'm eager to blister your bloodline. I've returned as blunt scythe to slit you into a new kind of man, heeled beneath the rough of my gaze.

each time you muscle me down this cobblestone, I scalp a sharper way up. and now you'll have to look at your tombed mistake, a gaunt exposure of what you thought you'd buried. you're running out of places to hide from me.

Author's Note: In the final line, "you're running out of places to hide from me" is from My Chemical Romance's "It's Not a Fashion Statement, It's a Fucking Deathwish."

the tailor

by

BISHAKH S⊙M

The tailor hunkers down in her kiosk, between the fruit and veg merchant and the egg vendor. She's shrouded in threadbare cloth, aanchol draped around her shoulders.

Black tresses shot through with silver cascade down to her clavicle. Her nose ring glints and flashes in the afternoon sun.

A small crimson crescent moon marks the space between her eyebrows.

Her cast iron machine, bulbous as a black eggplant adorned with balance wheel, needle suspended above gold throat plate, sits at a small sewing table in the corner.

The tailor cuts a long swath from a bolt of saffron and honey-colored silk, spits a plume of betel juice out onto the street.

She aligns the edge of the strip to the frayed edge of vermilion fabric, pinning it at intervals.

She threads a small needle with gold thread.

She works her way along the border.

When she reaches the other edge of the cloth, she ties the thread in a triple knot, brings the thread to her mouth and bites.

Perched on a long board atop three milk tins : a small black iron, attached to a cable that climbs straight up into the kiosk ceiling and snakes back into the dark recesses.

The tailor lays out the cloth on the board, flattening and smoothing the new seam.

She gathers opposite edges of the cloth and brings them together, flat, and again in the opposite direction, folding it into a self-contained parcel,

She stretches her head out of her stall and calls out to the egg vendor, a small woman with hair shorn close to the scalp.

She wears a white sari, edged with powder blue.

She lifts herself off her haunches with an exhalation and an oath, circles around her rattan basket,

Piled high with a pyramid of eggs, and shuffles over to the tailor's kiosk.

The tailor presents, with both hands outstretched,

the newly-mended cloth to the egg vendor, who chirps and marvels at the luster of the new saffron border.

She holds the tailor's hand and promises her extra sweets next month at her daughter's wedding.

She says next time she will commission a wedding sari for herself, as she ambles back to her mat — for her marriage to death, she chortles.

The tailor cocks her head, squints, shields her eyes against the glare.

"Oh worshipper of beauty!" she shouts at you. "What are you gawping at?"

"Do you want to kiss these cracked lips?"

THE CAPTIVE PHOTOGRAPH

Ariella Aïsha Azoulay

IN MARCH 2019 Tamara Lanier filed a lawsuit against Harvard University and Peabody Museum for "wrongful seizure, possession and expropriation of photographic images" of her enslaved ancestors, Renty Taylor and his daughter Delia. After Lanier's mother passed away in 2010, she had started researching information on Papa Renty. An acquaintance called her attention to the existence of the daguerreotypes of her ancestors, which Elinor Reichlin, on staff at the Peabody, had found in 1976.

Reichlin's preliminary research showed that in 1850 Louis Agassiz had commissioned these daguerreotypes under the mantle of authority provided by his position at Harvard University. Photography was just at its beginning then, and he used the project to prove his polygenic theory: that different human races had evolved separately and that white people were superior to others. Thus, the plate daguerreotypes of Renty and Delia (alongside those seized during the same photographic sessions from other enslaved people—Drana, Alfred, Jack, George Fassena, and Jem) are unlike other daguerreotypes commissioned by enslavers, which aimed to portray slavery as a paternalistic and benevolent form of white rule. These images had a different purpose: to capture in silver plates the inherent "truth" of white superiority. Stripping Renty, Delia, and the others bare in front of the camera was part of Agassiz and his collaborators' plan: to let what they considered the naked truth of Black inferiority *imprint* itself directly from the bodies to the photographic plate, without the interference of clothing or other props that were frequently used in photographers' studios. "If it is a shock to see full frontal nudity in early American photography," writes photography scholar and curator Brian Wallis, "it is even more surprising to see it without the trappings of shame or sexual fantasy."

Until Lanier stepped forward and claimed that these were her ancestors, the daguerreotypes had been assumed to be the private property of Harvard University. That Lanier's multiple attempts to communicate with representatives of university institutions were rebuffed testifies to the gravity and endurance of the institutional afterlife of slavery. Harvard's dismissal of Lanier brings to mind Jewish German philosopher Walter Benjamin's observation that when history is written by the victorious at the expense of the victims and survivors, the spoils become "cultural treasures." Only the victorious are permitted to claim as legally theirs what was seized from others. The latter were deprived of their freedom and rights and continue to live under the institutional conditions that make their grievances go unheard. Should academic institutions base their ownership claim on the victors' justice?

Azoulay

In March 2021 Lanier's lawsuit was dismissed by a Massachusetts court. Though an appeal is pending, the court confirmed not only Harvard's ownership of the daguerreotypes, but also the terms and the stake of the case. The court's decision centered the question of possession: To whom does Renty Taylor's daguerreotype belong? Yet Harvard came to "possess" these photographs through a cultural logic of wealth, property, and ownership that flows directly from slavery and preserves its lingering presence in our own era. Against this logic, I propose that we ask different questions. What if we insist on treating Renty as the person who was used against his will for others to extract an image of his enslavement, rather than as the object that was seized from him? Then, we must ask, where and with whom will Renty find peace and recognition of his rights?

The history of object restitution offers some guidance here as a form of historical accountability. It reminds us that the photograph is a social document, rather than an object to be possessed. In their social contexts, both the taking of the daguerreotype and its continued ownership and display by Harvard University constitute crimes against humanity that need to be redressed. The daguerreotypes are not property that can be owned, but ancestors who need caretaking. This understanding is the only way forward if we wish to repair the harms of enslavement.

IMAGINE IF RENTY'S RELATIVES, who likely heard no word from him after he was kidnapped from the Congo and enslaved in the United

States, could have had the opportunity to see his likeness alongside the millions of Americans celebrating the newly invented medium of the daguerreotype. We must question the privileges accorded to both scholars and the general public as viewers of these daguerreotypes. Instead of privileging their gaze, we should prioritize Renty's relatives, in both Africa and the United States. Indeed, daguerreotypes were invented and perceived by millions to keep dear ones close to their hearts and in their homes.

In the 1850s American writer, scientist, and former Dean of Harvard Medical School Oliver Wendell Holmes described the daguerreotype as a "mirror with memory." It is cruelly ironic that, during the same year that Agassiz revoked Renty and Delia's rights to participate in the gifting of these "mirrors with memory" to their relatives, Holmes, known for his racist eugenics theories, revoked the admission of the first three Black students to Harvard Medical School. Not only does Harvard now keep these daguerreotypes from the relatives waiting to hold them, it also shaped the white supremacist principle on which photography was institutionalized and millions were enslaved. In holding these images as part of its archival and museal capital, Harvard also invites millions to view Renty, Delia, and others not as ancestors or relatives, but as enslaved people.

Today we face an urgent need to draw a clear line between scholarship and the perpetuation of violence—the latter of which can be partially repaired by attending to the voices, grievances, and claims of those who were excluded from participating in public debates about the regimes that enslaved them. Further, we need to attend to the way that practices such as photography have been

Azoulay

shaped. We have the opportunity now—amid a wealth of scholarship and activism on the entanglement of photography, museums, and slavery, and based on increasing numbers of restitution cases—to redress what Renty and his relatives were deprived of in the 1850s. We have the opportunity for the unique imprint of Renty's presence on a silver plate to finally find its place where it belongs—with his family.

WE ARE ASKING QUESTIONS about the restitution of objects as part of an accountability process following totalitarian regimes—which I would argue include the American governments under which Africans were enslaved. An interesting parallel to consider is that the United States committed to restituting objects plundered from the Jews by the Nazis and their collaborators, notably the Vichy regime in France. Europe's postwar governments also embraced a fundamental principle of restitution. Two early examples are the 1950s German Restitution Laws and the French ordinance of April 21, 1945, which enabled victims, survivors, and their heirs to claim confiscated and looted property. Dating from the years following World War II, these laws are still used to bring justice internationally.

One of the latest examples involves property held in the United States. In 2017 a French court ordered an American couple to return a Camille Pisarro painting they had purchased in 1995. Unknown to the new owners, the painting had been plundered from its original Jewish owner, whose heirs were living in France.

The importance the U.S. government accorded to restitution at the end of World War II is indicated by the special military corps of British and American historians, curators, art scholars, and museum directors called "Monuments, Fine Arts and Archives." Known as the "Monuments Men," they are tasked with locating plundered art across Europe, tracking its provenance, and pursuing its just restitution to the original, primarily Jewish, owners.

Restitution was also mentioned in the Nuremberg Trials of Nazi leadership led by the former Allied powers, which sought to indict perpetrators for their crimes against humanity. The category "crimes against humanity" played a central role in the trials and was refined further in the years after. German Jewish political philosopher Hannah Arendt significantly impacted how the term is understood today. In her two major books, *The Origins of Totalitarianism* (1951) and *Eichmann in Jerusalem* (1963), Arendt analyzed specific Nazi practices and explained what distinguished them as crimes against humanity; but she also made clear that this type of crime was not reserved solely for Jews nor perpetrated solely by Nazis. Arendt argued that a polity whose laws were used in the process of committing crimes against humanity has an obligation to repair the social and political foundations of their laws. The only way to do this is to definitively end the lasting consequences of these crimes.

As an Arab-Jewish scholar myself, working in the tradition of Hannah Arendt, I feel a personal commitment to ensuring that redress, restitution, and repair are not solely the province of Jewish victims of crimes against humanity. Such an approach further exceptionalizes Jews at our own and other marginalized groups' expenses.

We should hold Euro-American institutions to the same standard of reparation for violence for all victims.

IN TODAY'S SCHOLARSHIP and in the practice of archives and museums, it is widely acknowledged that photographs are not discrete items that can be "owned" or understood outside the context of their production—that is, the reasons they were taken, the power relationships between the photographer and the photographed, and the initial forms of use and display. Put differently, given the different lives and afterlives of photographs, one cannot assume that a photograph is just a photograph.

This is not just a contemporary belief. Throughout the history of photography, and certainly in its first decades when Agassiz ordered these daguerreotypes to be taken, questions about the nature of the daguerreotype, its ownership, and its proper usage were answered differently by diverse actors and institutions. It was never a given that the photograph belonged to the person who took it or the hands that happened to hold the plate or the print.

Photographs taken under circumstances of violence are not reducible to what is recorded in them, since the violence that enabled their creation does not disappear after the camera's shutter clicks. Photographs taken to support violent regimes or acts retain the original violence in the image; they continue to sustain the original act of violence well after the image was produced. Numerous artists, scholars, curators, museum directors, communities, activists, and statesmen have made this point, seeking to recover, bury, withdraw from circulation, or restitute objects, images, remains, and other items that have been plundered or seized by violent regimes and are now held as aesthetic commodities in museums.

Photographs are the outcome of an encounter between people —they are social objects—and their fate cannot be determined by the conditions of their original production. If photographs were produced through force and in service of a regime of violence, then their future should not be determined without hearing the victims and offering reparative justice to them, their heirs, or survivors of that regime. Participants in the photographic encounter, or their heirs and communities, should be heard and their wishes taken into account. What is recorded in photographs is not yet over; redress is possible, and justice can still be granted.

THE DAGUERREOTYPES of Renty and Delia cannot be discussed with the legal terms usually reserved for photographs, as they could only have been produced as part of a regime that perpetrated crimes against humanity. Enslavement is recognized today by the United Nations and by International Law (Article 7, the Rome Statute of the International Criminal Court) as a crime against humanity. But slavery in the United States ended without any kind of proceeding akin to the Nuremberg trials, in which perpetrators were indicted and punished, and reparations and restitution followed. Though efforts were made to recompense formerly enslaved people during the early

Reconstruction era, this was an uneven and failed process that never involved the specific mandates around restitution and reparations that followed in the wake of World War II.

Although the punishment of individual perpetrators is no longer relevant here, the term "crime against humanity"—introduced in Nuremberg by the chief prosecutor in the trials, U.S. Associate Supreme Court Justice Robert Jackson—is still relevant here to understand the necessity of the restitution of these daguerreotypes.

Since the end of World War II, prominent political theory and legal scholars have attempted to parse the broader ethical, cultural, and legal aspects of this category. In her discussion, Arendt quotes Telford Taylor, counsel for the prosecution at the Nuremberg trials, who emphasized that these crimes are "not committed only against the victim, but primarily against the community whose law is violated." Arendt concluded that it is "the body politic itself that stands in need of being 'repaired'." In 2004 legal professor David Luban clarified that these actions constitute crimes, not wrongs, because they "violate important community norms." Thus, Luban argues, the community has the need and right "to vindicate those norms independently of the victim."

Arendt elucidates another major aspect of "crimes against humanity": the creation of a racial order aiming to physically and/or politically eliminate groups of people from the shared world. This organized attack on human diversity is an attack, Arendt argues, "upon a characteristic of the 'human status' without which the very words 'mankind' or 'humanity' would be devoid of meaning." As a regime, slavery created a world in which white people led and ran the different spheres of life, while Black people were eliminated as actors. But most white people did not perceive this as a crime. They did not view as crimes kidnapping, selling, purchasing, and forcing Black people to do different tasks; subjecting them to physical and psychological violence; or treating human beings as property. This owed to the regime of white supremacy and the belief in Black people's natural inferiority, inflected with patriarchy and the subjugation of Black women in particular—a belief that Agassiz sought to uphold when he ordered the forcibly nude photographs of Renty, Delia, and others. In this way, even white people who did not directly enslave Black people saw them as *potential* slaves or as fugitive slaves who had to be returned to their "owners." A world in which only white people were allowed to determine who could be property and what constituted a crime—and where the harm of non-whites was imperceptible to the system of law they enacted—constitutes a sustained attack against human diversity.

That the victims' skin color is what made the crimes against them imperceptible in the eyes of the white inhabitants of Columbia, South Carolina, where the daguerreotypes were seized from Renty and Delia, is one of the signs of a crime against humanity. Making this crime recognizable and nameable—rather than unacknowledged and imperceptible according to enslavers' laws—is at stake here.

Agassiz did not act in a vacuum; he was not a lone scholar pursuing an unpopular project. He was inspired by his professor Georges Cuvier, who worked at the Musée national d'Histoire naturelle in Paris and had access to the body of the enslaved Khoikhoi woman

Sara Saartjie Baartman, who was publicly presented using the racist and pejorative name "Hottentot Venus." Cuvier used Baartman's body as proof of his theories of scientific racism. After her death he conducted an autopsy of her body and "proved" that her remains were markedly different from European corpses. Agassiz was also likely in regular contact with Samuel Morton, with whom he could discuss how the new technology of the daguerreotype might be used to prove his theories of scientific racism. Morton himself had a vast collection of skulls ("the American Golgotha") which he used for the racial science of phrenology, proving the evolutionary superiority of some races over others through studying the skull. Other scientists and enslavers gave Agassiz inspiration and guidance or were directly involved in the production of his daguerreotype images. For example, a local physician, Robert W. Gibbs, used his plantation contacts and visits to select enslaved "subjects" of an ideal "type" for Agassiz's photographs.

IN THE EYES OF THE WHITE MEN who planned the photographic session, Renty, Delia, Drana, Alfred, Jack, George, and Jem were considered less than human. It was not their likeness that Harvard's scholar sought to produce during the photographic session. Rather, the aim was to generate visual proofs that could justify the enslavement of Black people. This distinction is quite important: Agassiz, Zealy, and the others involved did not take photographs *of* slaves, but rather forced Renty, Delia, Drana, Alfred, Jack, George, and Jem to be photographed *as* slaves. Under the pretext that photographs carry an objective truth, these daguerreotypes were made to force Black people to stay captives of slavery, and serve as proof of their innate potential for enslavement. The white men could seize these images because the photographic subjects were enslaved, thus the images seized were of the subjects' enslavement. The photographer's camera was part of what literary critic Hortense Spillers describes as the "tortures and instruments of captivity."

For too long, the images seized from Renty and the others were presented and discussed as images *of* slaves, ignoring the power of photography to prolong the status of "slave" forced on the photographed persons—the perpetuation, following Arendt, of a crime against humanity. In all its publications and interpretations, Harvard denies the simple truth of the matter: as long as spectators possess the right to view the photographed persons in scenes of captivity—with the photographs handled as if they are the museum's property—Black people will forever be presented as "slaves." This is yet another example of the violent afterlife of slavery.

But Harvard skirts this truth, instead positioning itself as a spectator who can "free" the photographed persons from their captivity. The statements Harvard has offered on the photographs position the institution as a white savior with the right to "preserve" this horror lest people forget—ignoring entirely the descendants of slavery and the fact that they never forgot their enslavement, as Lanier's demand examplifies. Restituting these daguerreotypes to descendants, who are also survivors of this regime of slavery, accomplishes far more than displaying them to white audiences ever will.

Harvard's various proposals of how best to exhibit the images —emphasizing the "reciprocal gaze" of those whose images have been seized, presenting the photographs in pedagogical settings not as "types" but as "portraits"—are creative and inventive, but they cannot address the simple truth of Lanier's claim. In Lanier's claim, voiced by an heir who sees Renty as her ancestor, the paradox collapses. Renty is not in need of any savior, and certainly not by the institution that seized his image in the first place; he just needs to go home.

At home the image could perhaps be kept as people do images of their relatives: touched by hands, worn, forgotten, recalled, shown to others. Images get stained, placed in drawers, retrieved, lost, invoked in conversations and used to spark longing, even as their colors and contrasts fade away. But the proximity of the nakedness of enslavement might guide Lanier to touch this daguerreotype differently. The last thing Harvard's experts should do after the photograph's restitution is ask Lanier her plans for the daguerreotype. It is exactly the end of this reminder of enslavers' right to determine how descendants of slavery are allowed to mourn or celebrate their ancestors that the Taylors' reunification with Lanier could achieve.

A decision to allow Renty to go home might raise questions about how this might pertain to other objects held in Harvard's museums and archives, and in similar institutions in the West. But it will not create a precedent, since precedents have already been created. Objects are constantly being restituted, including those plundered by the circle of Agassiz. The University of Pennsylvania announced its plans to repatriate human skulls from Morton's collection, including several of the skulls of enslaved people. The museum director, Christopher Woods, said, "An initial phase of rigorous evaluation was critical for ensuring an ethical and respectful process around repair." At the request of Nelson Mandela during his first year as president of an apartheid-free country, Sara Baartman's body was restituted to South Africa and buried there. The French returned skulls of Algerian warriors they had seized in 1849. The Humboldt Forum in Berlin has recently announced its plans to restitute some of the Benin Bronzes, seized by British forces from West Africa in the nineteenth century. For more than seventy-five years, Jewish property has been restituted in the wake of Nazi expropriation and looting. And the list continues.

The whole idea behind the category of crimes against humanity, as was made clear in Nuremberg and since, was to create a legal precedent—not to be used to secure unjust gains, but to prevent such crimes from being committed again. These objects were seized as part of a regime that perpetrated crimes against humanity. The day that Tamara Lanier recognized in Renty not as "a slave" but as her great-great-great-grandfather, she invited members of the community to join her efforts to free her ancestors from captivity in a world in which their status as slaves was being prolonged, their freedom not fully recognized, and their rights not yet redressed.

IN PHOTOGRAPHY'S FIRST DECADES, when these daguerreotypes were taken, photographers did not have exclusive property rights to the images they produced. Harvard's lawyers argue, "the rule is that a photograph is the property of the photographer, not the subject, and there are cases that we've cited in our brief that apply that rule even in cases when the subject of the images did not consent to the images being captured." But this imposes one conception of photography retroactively on a complex history composed of competing claims about ownership and rights.

Visitors to photographers' studios purchased the daguerreotypes produced by their presence in front of the camera—*their* daguerreotypes—and held them as property. On much less frequent occasions, photographers produced additional plates from the same pose and kept them, but this was largely permissible since the ownership of daguerreotypes was not yet standardized. That photographs taken of others, including photographs taken in their own studios, were automatically the property of the photographer was not guaranteed even when a case went to court.

For example, in 1860, Louis-Auguste Bisson, official photographer of Napoléon III, was commissioned by painter Adolphe Yvon to take the emperor's photograph for Yvon to use as a model for one of his paintings. When the painter realized that Bisson had printed many copies of the commissioned photograph, he feared that it would devalue his painting; he sued the photographer, and won. The court ruled that the photograph was Yvon's property, not the photographer's.

I don't raise this as a precedent to legally determine who has property rights in photographs, but to remind us that the ownership of photographic images was undecided and in a state of flux at that time. This is still the case in our own time, as the debates over image banks or archives of colonial violence in former empires exemplify today. Photographs transcend any idea of private property and cannot be dealt with in these limited terms.

Photographs are the outcome of different people coming together under different circumstances. These situations cannot be assessed using a single model since the "photographic event"—as I call this coming together of people—varies greatly, from relations of love, consent, and exchange to exploitation, coercion, and violence. Photographs transcend the question of simple ownership because the object itself was produced, seized, circulated, and used in ways that violated others' rights. We are not solely dealing with the right of one party to own a certain object, but the rights of the other parties involved in the photographic encounter.

After abolition, many individuals and institutions who acquired their wealth through slavery did not question that they had done so by turning Black people into property, rendering Black people propertyless, and expropriating the fruits of their labor. Those who profited from slavery were not challenged in the decades following abolition. Thus, their heirs have assumed that the wealth they inherited is rightly theirs or that their privileged access to it should be secured. Whenever this injustice enters the courtroom, it creates an opportunity to remedy it—for the sake of its direct victims first, but also to free the heirs of perpetrators from structural and institutional complicity in perpetuating their ancestors' violence by not stopping the lingering effects of the crimes against humanity carried out in their society. Rejecting Lanier's genuine demand to let her ancestors exit the museum, Harvard not only rejects the grievance of a descendant of slavery, but asks all of us to refuse to see slavery's crimes against humanity and their lingering presence.

These daguerreotypes of Renty and Delia are not property and are not Harvard's property. Even after they are restituted to Lanier, they will not be *her* property: they will be under her custody or guardianship. These daguerreotypes should not have been taken. But they were taken, and they do exist. So, we should think about them as we would think about a family member who needs caretaking from close relatives.

The question of kinship here is primary. Lanier and Harvard are not equal parties debating ownership over a piece of property. These daguerreotypes were seized from Renty and Delia in a world in which, as Spillers describes it, "flesh [was] for sale, flesh [was] summed up as a medium of exchange." Describing the transition from enslaved to free, Spillers counts "touch" as the first sense to be engaged after freedom:

> Touch may be the first measure of what it means not to be enchained anymore. When I can declare my body as my own space and when you have to gain permission from me implicitly to put your hands on me, I think it makes a difference.

We do not know and do not need to know the details leading to the photographed persons posing naked to assume that they did not consent to be in the photographs, to be seen by those whites who trafficked in their flesh, or to be seen by us. What we do know is that these daguerreotypes are the outcome of violence and cannot be approached as ordinary photographs.

Lanier claims that Harvard has no right to continue to touch her great-great-great-grandfather, to force him to be half nude in front of a public gaze. Under slavery, Spillers writes, "kinship loses meaning, since it can be invaded at any given and arbitrary moment by the property relations." Denying Harvard the property rights to what was stolen from her great-great-great-grandfather and his kin is a way to repair kinship for Lanier, wounded by the long afterlife of slavery. "If 'kinship' were possible," Spillers continues, "the property relations would be undermined." If not then—now.

Expanding the conversations about ethical approaches to collections formed under regimes of violence pushes museums today to "deal with claims for the restitution of artefacts and the repatriation of human remains," as German museum studies scholar Larissa Förster writes. This distinction is crucial in the case of Renty and Delia, as narrowing the question to solely focus on the restitution of museum items accepts the terms imposed by the museum, and the terms involved in their captivity. Lanier, in saying "this is my ancestor," not a museum asset, also demands repatriation. Renty and Delia were forced to enter a museum collection and Lanier demands they be repatriated to where they belong: among their relatives.

This demand finds justification in the fact that these daguerreotypes turned museum objects could not have been seized without Renty and others first being kidnapped into slavery. The light reflected from their naked bodies and captured in daguerreotype plates was also abducted. Any technical or scientific explanation of the procedure of the daguerreotype cannot ignore that these would not exist without the subjects being forced to have a portion of their naked skin open to the light and reflected onto the sensitive surface of these plates. These daguerreotypes are, in a literal sense, the remains of their presence, forced enslavement, and unwilling nudity.

Given this history, Harvard should have immediately renounced any claims of ownership to these images. But the university still has the opportunity to encourage Black people to consult its archives and restore their connection to kin that Harvard has in its holdings, and work to ensure that all its faculty and students learn from Lanier. Harvard now has the opportunity not only for restitution and repair, but to further its pedagogical and scholarly mission along these lines.

WHEN RENTY, Delia, and the others were forced to go to Zealy's studio, they didn't encounter a photographer who wanted to interact with them to produce their likeness. They encountered another enslaver, invested in the regime of slavery, for whom there was nothing more obvious than the fact that they were slaves and must be made to surrender their bodies to perpetuate their plight. (Zealy counted six Black people as his property.) The entire session at the photographer's studio, involving several white people, was devoted to producing visual proof that Renty, Delia, and the others were who the enslavers and profiteers wanted them to be: slaves.

This was possible because the regime of slavery relied on creating a society of peers who recognized not only the right of whites to enslave Blacks, but also the potential of each new technology to reaffirm the regime—a society of peers whose crimes against humanity are, for the perpetrators, rendered imperceptible, "natural." This imperceptibility is materialized in these daguerreotypes; since their creation, viewers have been asked to recognize "the absolute power of masters over the bodies of their slaves," here obliged to pose naked.

And the imperceptibility of the crime to the eyes of perpetrators still persists, exemplified by Harvard and the Peabody Museum's expectation that Renty, Delia, and the others continue to provide scientific proofs with their bodies—now in the service of Harvard's "educational mission" and the institution's self-study. As artist Carrie Mae Weems said, these daguerreotypes stand for the way "Anglo America—white America—saw itself in relationship to the Black subject." This is true not only in what could be seen in the daguerreotypes, but in the institution's obstinate denial to recognize Lanier as the heir of Renty and his kin.

RESTITUTION DEMANDS that we hear from different places and people, attend to the provenance of items in our museums, and question their status as "private property." Restitution asks that we consider these items in museums to be the ancestors of the communities from which they were taken, part of a life-world that was destroyed through the process of colonization, enslavement, or plunder. This was the premise of the 1990 U.S. federal Native American Graves Protection and Repatriation Act (NAGPRA), and it is repeated all over the world. As two recent articles on the repatriation of the Benin Bronzes illustrate, art held in museums is not property to those from whom it was taken, but ancestors: headlines read "'They're not property': the people who want their ancestors back from British museums" (the *Guardian*) and "In the West, the Looted Bronzes are Museum Pieces. In Nigeria, 'They Are Our Ancestors'" (the *New York Times*).

Renty never owned the daguerreotype that was seized from him. To have been in a position to take ownership of it would've first required that he not be enslaved, and then the daguerreotype would have never been brought into existence anyway. What was seized from him is congealed in the photographic image itself—it is a remnant of his presence, an imprint of his flesh interacting with light, that Harvard continues to claim as a museum asset. "He is my ancestor," Lanier argues, not your "medium of exchange." Lanier claims the restitution of the object, but expects the repatriation of her ancestor's remains.

MAMABIRD

fiction by aureleo sans

IT WAS WINTER in the projects when Vega first felt her heart flutter. Christmas lights strangled aloe vera plants and weatherworn flamingos. Everything here was muted including the color of the residents' skin with one exception: Tio Eusebio and his stash of Natural White and White Radiance creams imported from Barranquilla. He said they helped restore his natural complexion.

"It's in the quicksilver," he proclaimed.

Truth was everything was fading. The blue sky was gray, and outside Vega's window the ice cream truck Yankee Doodled, and the mourning doves sounded like they were choking.

Vega's grandparents ferried her to Dr. Sonora to make sure she didn't fade too soon. Dr. Sonora with the glasses that inflated his eyes to anime proportions. Before he could ask, she told him the flutter was not love. (At least not like when Felipe stuck his dick in her.) It was something serious. The doctor asked her if she exercised and she snorted. Is this bitch for real? She might be small, but she's definitely not a cheerleader-type with a thigh gap. Her appetite for Dairy Queen Blizzards and Little Caesars Crazy Bread was palpable. Grandma said as much. It was true that PE was a required course, but because the coach didn't want to do shit, he only had them walk around the track twice every other day, which was tiring but that wasn't exercise, not really. No, she wasn't on any meds. She wasn't doing no illegal drugs either. She wasn't pregnant. She wasn't sexually active. She wasn't depressed. She didn't miss her biological parents. She lied lied lied. She didn't appreciate the third degree or how Grandma side-eyed her during the third degree and then, when they got home, interrogated her like she was the law, going down the list of all of the illegal substances she knew, which was three. The doctor said her heart was ticking good. He diagnosed her with generalized anxiety disorder. She and Grandma didn't know why the name was so long when she just had a case of the nerves.

From that day forward, whenever she mentioned the palpitations, Grandma would sour and yell, "No seas tan histérica," because Vega was interrupting the latest episode of *La Usurpadora* and hadn't Grandma sacrificed enough by cleaning toilets all day and then cooking—which was really microwaving, but Vega wasn't going to say it—and cleaning some more. So Vega stopped talking about it, but she was scared. Inside her, tumbleweeds tumbled one day, and the next, sneakers somersaulted in a dryer.

Maybe her heart was trying and failing to speak. Maybe it was transmitting Morse code warnings about Felipe. Maybe it was screaming, "Break up, Vega, before it is too late." Maybe it was too late, and maybe she was pregnant, and the baby wasn't none too smart like Felipe and decided to live too close to her heart.

She gulped the air while Abuelo sat in front of a different TV watching the Cowboys and *King of Queens* and drinking and pretending not to hear most things. The doctor gave her an Rx for Klonopin. The pills were magic school buses.

She knew she was nothing new. Around here there was something wrong with everyone: Stacy and the wooly caterpillar unibrow that she razored away every couple months, Cynthia who tossed her secrets and her aluminum cans into a black garbage bag she carried everywhere. The bag metastasized until it was even with the second-floor roof, and the city bus driver stopped letting her sit the bag on top of his bus because of "liability reasons," and the bag was confiscated and labeled an undesirable occupant, and she was evicted. Renee and her dog Trudy, both with moonstone eyes they called cataracts. Diego always running away from everyone because demons were running after him until eventually they threw him and the demons into a jail cell because you can't run away from life, and you certainly can't run away from the police. Chuy, the street artist, and his graffiti figures, Snoop Dogg, Bugs Bunny, El Gato del Raval, and Yolanda Saldívar, who sold kids dime bags of brown and white and played shell games at the bus stop. And Radioactive Roxanne, always flashing the streets during the day and the skies at night.

No one questions the way things are. No one questions poverty. No one questions the body (except doctors) because the body is mute and dumb, and there are too many plausible reasons and too many plausible villains to justify diagnoses and calamities. It could've been all of the things. Decades earlier the Air Force stippled the land with pits and deposited chemicals used to lift grease and strip paint, casting a plume of toxicity that sat below the surface and fueled an epidemic of cancer and asthma; Vega thought the word, "plume," was poetic. Vega's parents had been drug addicts and she'd been a preemie and they'd given her up and then they'd given life up and once she heard her grandparents tell the school counselor about "birth defects," but how could anyone call a part of a human being a defect? Tio Eusebio always shook her hand with his hand coated with the lightening cream residue and its toxic metals as if to suggest she too needed to bleach. The neighborhood's families, unable to cope with the indignities of living without, swapped their food stamps and WIC cheese for a diet of vices and candy. After each tenant eviction, the landlord spackled a new coat of the cheapest paint on top of the old, so that there was more paint (and lead) on the wall than substrate and infants like Vega ate paint chips like potato chips. Hell, Vega with her long nails would still chip away at the paint for a snack. It calmed her. It tasted like home.

So, when the chorus of chirping made its debut, Vega knew something was wrong but she also thought it was another one of those unwanted facts of life she had to live with. And so every morning she woke up first to the fluttering in her chest and then to an internal birdsong, which was a better soundtrack anyhow than the train's song two blocks away every couple hours. For a time, she was a passerine radio station.

The boys at school had always called her "special." The girls didn't talk to her, but they didn't know she had smarts even though she couldn't count change because who uses coins anyway, and she had no interest in Shakespeare. Her favorite teacher was that crazy white lady, Ms. Moon, who taught biology. Hair stuck out of her ears, and crazy struck out of her eyes. One day, Vega's favorite day so far at school, Ms. Moon announced that that morning when she'd woke the bodies of sparrows with their feet up like dead roaches had blanketed her front lawn, maybe it was acid rain or bird flu, and so she'd scooped them up, organized them into two shoeboxes, and dusted them with Triazicide, which sounded like a crime.

"And here they are, class!"

She opened the boxes like treasure chests. Two girls ran out crying, but most of the students crowded around in awe. She then let each student select a bird. Their bodies plopped on trays like lunchroom lasagna. She passed out tweezers and scalpels and assigned the students to pluck and skin and dissect the carcasses. Vega was the first to discover that inside each dead bird was a tiny diamond, and Ms. Moon let the students keep each and every one.

But life always spirals out of control like a mutated double helix, and Vega thought maybe this was the revenge of the diamond sparrows because eventually the birdsong in her chest raised its voice and Ms. Moon heard it, cocked her head to one side and then the other, listening, maybe trying to identify the bird call, and then removed her from the classroom.

"You know the rules, Vega," Ms. Moon said, shaking her nest of hair, dandruff snowflakes flying. "No electronic devices at school. Please hand it over."

Vega pleaded with her eyes, then rolled them. How could she explain her life to a white lady? She silently reversed her pockets, and Ms. Moon looked even more aggro, gave her a perfunctory "last chance to come clean," and then banished her to in-school suspension, which wasn't fair, but by the time she got to the ISS room the morning burst of bird song had subsided and she stared blankly at the white cinderblock walls and ignored Jose and Eric miming chickens and dogs.

After that incident, she stopped going to school, and nobody cared. Abuelo told her that if she wasn't going to school, she was going to need to get a job if she wanted to live in his house and that no one was going to support a desgraciada but then he dropped the subject, and no one seemed to have heard.

Sometimes it felt like her rib cage was going to burst. Her body shrieked and screeched and squalled in pain, and she went over to Felipe's to drown herself in sex but he'd get tired and let up and then her chest hurt again. People said you can learn how to dissociate from your body. Stacy said sometimes when her stepdad came into the room she watched from the ceiling what he did to her. Vega wished for that power.

And that's when it happened: a titmouse escaped from her mouth. She had never seen one before. He looked like a miniature cardinal robbed of color. The West Side only had pigeons, doves, sparrows, grackles, crows, blue jays, and cardinals, the last two like occasional flashes of the flag. The titmouse whistled to Vega, and she opened the window and he lingered, flittering, and then she made a shooing motion with her hands, and he flew away. She didn't want no trouble. But still he returned every morning outside her window to rejoin the chorus that emerged from her chest.

A swarm of warring hummingbirds erupted next. One after the other until they filled the room, an invasion of jewels: rubies, emeralds, amethysts, topazes, and tanzanites like on the Home Shopping Network but these buzzed and moved until they began flying in reverse and wheeling and dealing and colliding and scrapping with one another because there was no more space and one crashed to the ground and Vega screamed. They say their hearts beat at 1,200 beats a minute, and maybe one of their hearts had stopped beating.

Abuelo opened the door and said, "This better be good because the Masked Singer is on," and then, "What did you do?" and then, when he saw her on the floor crying, blood trickling from her lips, "Mija, are you OK?" He didn't seem too surprised though. He had heard the songs too.

Abuelo, notwithstanding his liver spots and his wartime limp, took command. He took a forty of Camo and went over to Barabbas's place. Barabbas was one of three neighborhood hoarders, and in his home, past collections of mismatched tires and Furbies, teetered columns of bird cages left over from his days catching city pigeons and then trying to convert them into carrier pigeons to sell on Craigslist. He said he had read an article, but we all knew about his periodic visits to the psych ward, and none of the pigeons, a flock of hundreds, stayed around long enough for his discharge date except one and the less said about Minerva the better because she always looked like she was on her last claw. Once when Vega had asked to go over Grandma had said, "That's how you get lice so leave that bird alone." The rest of Barabbas's flock never homed their way back home, although occasionally the neighbors found miniature scrolls that said, "Live Long and Prosper," or "I Don't Think You're Ready for This Jelly."

Minerva wasn't the only pigeon on the block after a passenger pigeon flew out of Vega's mouth. The purple of its neck blazed even after Vega announced her discovery and Abuelo got too excited with a fishermen's net and killed the bird, and the passenger pigeon went extinct again.

In his solid gold years, Abuelo had owned a hybrid tienda/icehouse, where he hatched unsuccessful get-rich-quick schemes: the virtual slot machines, the counterfeit money press, the backyard Chow Chow puppy mill, the artisanal psilocybin farm. Now he had found purpose again and began warehousing birds in cages.

"We've hit the jackpot, chick," he told Vega.

Using Barabbas's cages, he rounded up each bird for incarceration, then pecked at his keyboard to advertise his avian wares on Craigslist and OfferUp. Meanwhile, Vega, in between spurts of pain and feathers, flipped through a dog-eared field guide of birds and IDed the species: chats, chickadees, dickcissels, shrikes, larks, thrushes, thrashers, a flycatcher that tickled her tonsils, lazuli buntings, redstarts, red-winged blackbirds, blue blue bluebirds. She also IDed the customers: moms who couldn't say no to their children, flea market vendors, representatives of rural zoos whose lions, tigers, and bears mauled visitors every year, balding middle-aged men with paunches who bought things just to own them. They all looked hungry.

Grandma remained downstairs more glued than ever to the TV set. She'd been perturbed by all of the strange visits, the caked bird shit and feathers on the floor, the ongoing cacophony. Vega slipped downstairs and pleaded to go to the ER. The pain was so great.

"I am sure it's nothing," Grandma said. "Maybe you'll sprout wings of your own and fly away." She said this as a joke but no one laughed, not even the mynas.

Vega tried to remember providence and gratitude. At least it was the mouth and not her other openings. She had seen the video of a woman in Thailand with parakeets entering and exiting the vagina.

In so many ways, she could not even. Human mouths can open, on average and at most, two inches, and the birds kept growing in length and circumference. In desperate escape attempts, woodpecker beaks chipped at her enamel, compounding the ache. She was grateful no one tried to escape through her cheeks.

Flights of anxiety heightened the pain. She worried that her grandparents, who had evaded the detention centers, might be thrown in jail for violating the Migratory Bird Treaty Act. She worried that they might contract bird fancier's lung or, worse, parrot fever, and, in fact, they *did* contract the latter and when Barabbas carted them to the hospital, Vega was left alone with birds flowing out of her mouth like a hose, and no one to capture them so she opened a window, and that's when it happened, an anhinga breached her mouth, and Vega asphyxiated and died.

But her lifeless body still had life in it, and at her lips the seam of her body began to unzip. First, the anhinga peeled out and stood on the ledge outside the window, its wings outstretched drying in the sun like Jesus on the cross. Next, two zopilotes hopped out eyeing Vega's undulating flesh with admiration and concern. And then an albatross revealed. It brayed at the vultures, opened its impossible wingspan, and hugged her shapeshifting body. The final reveal was a flamingo white as snow. Vega's body was now shed snakeskin on the floor. The birds stared at each other, and then the anhinga flapped its wings and took flight and so did the rest of the flock except for the flamingo. She perched on the red roofs of the housing project with her beak open pecking at the raincloud grey air and feeding on the sadness that hung there like old clothes on a line. After a week, the bird turned black like charcoal briquettes like week-old gum on the sidewalk your index finger scratches and dips into your mouth like Grandma's hair smelling of Cashmere Bouquet like gas station grackles.

Every morning, the flamingo would tap on the windows of each apartment where an infant or elder lived. Into open mouths, the flamingo would dip her beak, her neck rippling. She fed the residents grit. She fed Grandma and Abuelo double, and every night they turned off the TV and busted out the boombox and held hands and took account of the new callouses and grooves running up and down their heart and life lines and their feet clip-clopped to cumbia. Years passed and the bird had cured cancer in the projects, rendered inert the plume and the lead and the heavy metals in Tio Eusebio's whitening cream, and vanquished the ultraviolence and the ultraviolet. Her sharp bill swiped guns from drunkards, and her flapping wings generated breeze and brilliance. She raised a generation, including a set of twins, who won Senate seats and then launched failed bids for president but still managed to expand the powers of the Migratory Bird Act to cover all birds, big and small.

CONTRIBUTORS

Kemi Alabi is author of *Against Heaven*, winner of the Academy of American Poets First Book Award, and coeditor of *The Echoing Ida Collection*. They live in Chicago.

Donia Elizabeth Allen's work has appeared in *Agni*, *jubilat*, and *Callaloo*. Allen holds an MFA in Poetry from Columbia, and an MA in Afro-American Studies from the University of Wisconsin-Madison.

Ariella Aïsha Azoulay is Professor of Modern Culture and Media in the Department of Comparative Literature at Brown University and author of *Potential History—Unlearning Imperialism*.

Don Mee Choi is author of the National Book Award–winning book *DMZ Colony*. She is a 2021 MacArthur and Guggenheim fellow.

Adebe DeRango-Adem attended the Jack Kerouac School of Disembodied Poetics (Naropa University). She is author of *Ex Nihilo*, *Terra Incognita*, and *The Unmooring*. She served as the 2019–20 Barbara Smith Writer-in-Residence with Twelve Literary Arts in Cleveland. Her fourth collection, *Vox Humana*, is forthcoming with Book*hug Press.

Emma Dries received her MFA in Fiction from Johns Hopkins University. Previously, she worked in editorial at Alfred A. Knopf, Doubleday, and Ecco Books. Her writing has been published in *Outside* and *Literary Hub*.

Farah Jasmine Griffin is Chair of African American and African Diaspora Studies, Director of the Institute for Research in African American Studies, and the William B. Ransford Professor of English and Comparative Literature and African American Studies at Columbia University. Her most recent book is *Harlem Nocturne: Women Artists and Progressive Politics During World War II*.

Randall Horton is author of the memoir *Dead Weight* and several books of poetry, including *Pitch Dark Anarchy* and *The Lingua Franca of Ninth Street*. He is the recipient of the Gwendolyn Brooks Poetry Award and is Professor of English at the University of New Haven.

Savonna Johnson teaches English Composition at the University of Pittsburgh. Her poetry has been featured in *Snapdragon: A Journal of Art & Healing* and on poets.org.

Kim Hyesoon is one of the most prominent contemporary poets of South Korea. Her recent poetry in translation, *Autobiography of Death*, won the 2019 International Griffin Poetry Prize.

Maya Marshall is author of *All the Blood Involved in Love*. The recipient of fellowships from Cave Canem, MacDowell, and Callaloo, she currently serves as the 2021–23 Poetry Fellow at Emory University.

Colleen Murphy is the Roger and Stephany Joslin Professor of Law and Professor of Philosophy and Political Science at the University of Illinois at Urbana-Champaign. A Public Voices Fellow with The Op-Ed Project, she is author of *The Conceptual Foundations of Transitional Justice* and *A Moral Theory of Political Reconciliation*.

Simone Person is a two-time Pink Door Writing Retreat fellow and editor for *just femme & dandy*. Their prose chapbook *Dislocate* won the Honeysuckle Press 2017 Chapbook Contest, and their poetry chapbook *Smoke Girl* won the Diode Editions 2018 Chapbook Contest and the 2020 Eric Hoffer Book Award (Chapbook).

aureleo sans is a VONA alumnus, a 2022 Tin House Scholar, and a 2022 Periplus fellow. His work has been published in *Passages North*, *Electric Literature*, *Shenandoah*, the *Masters Review*, and *Fractured Lit*, where he won second place in the 2021 Micro Fiction Contest.

Bishakh Som's work has appeared in the *New Yorker*, *Autostraddle*, the *Strumpet*, *Black Warrior Review*, and the *Brooklyn Rail*. Her graphic novel *Apsara Engine* is the winner of a 2021 *L.A. Times* Book Prize for Best Graphic Novel and a 2021 Lambda Literary Award winner for Best LGBTQ Comics. Her graphic memoir *Spellbound* was also a 2021 Lambda Literary Award finalist.

Olúfẹ́mi O. Táíwò is Assistant Professor of Philosophy at Georgetown University and author of *Reconsidering Reparations*.

Meredith Talusan is author of the memoir *Fairest*, a finalist for the Lambda Literary Award, and has written for the *New York Times*, the *Guardian*, the *Atlantic*, *LitHub*, *Guernica*, *Catapult*, and contributed to the fiction collection *Anonymous Sex*. Meredith teaches in the MFA programs at Antioch College and Sarah Lawrence College.

Brian Teare is a 2020 Guggenheim Fellow and author of six critically acclaimed books, most recently *Companion Grasses*, *The Empty Form Goes All the Way to Heaven*, and *Doomstead Days*, winner of the Four Quartets Prize. He is Associate Professor at the University of Virginia and makes books by hand for his micropress, Albion Books.

Yiru Zhang has work in *Reed Magazine*, the *Florida Review*, *Tahoma Literary Review*, and *Gordon Square Review*. In her native Chinese, she has works published in *Taiwan and Hong Kong Literature*, *Fiction World*, and elsewhere. A finalist for the John Steinbeck Award for Fiction and a recipient of the Literary Journal's New Criticism Award, she works as a literary reporter and translates American short stories into Chinese.